A Man Set Free

By John Butterworth
Written in cooperation with Bill Smith and World Wide Crusades

A true story of God's deliverance from sin, self and prison bars that allowed one man to find his part in the Kingdom of God and another man to find a faithful friend and fellow laborer in proclaiming the good news about Jesus Christ.

Printed in Victoria, Canada

Scripture quotations marked NKJV are from the New King James Version, copyright 1982 and 1990 by Thomas Nelson, Inc.

Scripture quotations marked as KJV are from the 1769 Authorized Version, commonly called the King James Version, public domain outside the U.K.

Scripture quotations marked as NASB are from the New American Standard Bible, copyright the Lockman Foundation 1960, 1962, 1963, 1968, 1971, 1973, 1975, 1977, 1980.

Note for Librarians: a cataloguing record for this book that includes Dewey Classification and US Library of Congress numbers is available from the National Library of Canada. The complete cataloguing record can be obtained from the National Library's online database at:
www.nlc-bnc.ca/amicus/index-e.html

ISBN 1-4120-2573-7

TRAFFORD

This book was published on-demand in cooperation with Trafford Publishing.
On-demand publishing is a unique process and service of making a book available for retail sale to the public taking advantage of on-demand manufacturing and Internet marketing. On-demand publishing includes promotions, retail sales, manufacturing, order fulfilment, accounting and collecting royalties on behalf of the author.

Suite 6E, 2333 Government St., Victoria, B.C. V8T 4P4, CANADA
Phone   250-383-6864   Toll-free   1-888-232-4444 (Canada & US)
Fax   250-383-6804   E-mail   sales@trafford.com
Web site www.trafford.com   TRAFFORD PUBLISHING IS A DIVISION OF TRAFFORD HOLDINGS LTD.
Trafford Catalogue #04-0401   www.trafford.com/robots/04-0401.html
10   9   8   7   6   5   4   3

C O N T E N T S

Preface

About The Author

I first met the man known to the California State Prison System as Ricardo Fuentes in 2000 at the airport in Managua, Nicaragua. I was in that country not only as part of an evangelistic outreach, but also as a reporter for the Corvallis Gazette-Times, an Oregon newspaper in the Willamette Valley. I had already been to Central America once with another group led by Bill Smith, an Assembly of God pastor from a small church in Alsea, Oregon. During that trip, Smith led a group of about a dozen volunteers to Honduras after Hurricane Mitch had shredded the lives and infrastructure of Honduras and Nicaragua. The goal then was to help build a new church building in one of San Pedro Sula's suburbs (a less than accurate term for some of the areas developing outside of the city's boundaries), start a new church ministry in another area of the city and hold medical clinics in some of the incredibly poor areas away from San Pedro Sula.

While we were in Honduras helping others, Ricardo Fuentes was locked up in a California penitentiary.

A year or so later, we arrived in Nicaragua the day after the country's national elections and two days before the national elections in the United States that would see the results battled clear to the Supreme Court. Nicaraguans faced a similar turn around in the election results to that of the Al Gore-George W. Bush controversy, but they handled things differently than their counterparts to the north.

After claiming our baggage at the airport, Fuentes told us we needed to ride in the back of his truck across the four-lane highway to the motel where we'd spend the night. It was not safe to be out on the streets, he said. We'd later hear reports that in the northern town of Jalapa, our destination for a four-day evangelistic crusade, residents had rioted, turned over cars to blockade streets and two men had died in the chaos.

With that unsettling news, the next day we spent several hours in a small boat of questionable dependability on Lago de Nicaragua.

Interestingly enough, and it seemed almost fitting to me given the state of unrest in the nation, the lake supports a rare species of fresh water sharks. It was on that boat trip to a small island restaurant for a taste of real Nicaraguan food that I first heard the story of Fuentes' life.

A year later during another crusade with Smith, this time in El Jicaro, Nicaragua, I'd learn more of the miraculous story of the power of God's grace manifested to this man pulled from the dregs of society and converted to be used for proclaiming the gospel of Jesus Christ in Central America by an English speaking evangelist.

My hopes and prayers in the writing of this book is that those who don't know that God came in the flesh of Jesus Christ, the only begotten Son of God, to provide the cure and pay the penalty for our own sins, as well as provide us the power through his Holy Spirit to live a life that conquers the desire for fame, fortune, power and pleasure that has drawn the rest of the world into an ever downward spiraling abyss, will see him as the God who is. For those who already know this Jesus Christ as Lord and Savior, I pray that they'll be drawn closer to God and encouraged to boldly proclaim his name as they read the testimony in these pages.

In producing A Man Set Free, my goal is to provide for the continuing support of the World Wide Crusades ministry and its efforts to reach out to more of those who have not heard of the good news of Jesus Christ.

As Fuentes would one day end up praying, "Lord, be your will done."

– John Butterworth, June 2003

A journalist, photographer and adventurer, John Butterworth spent from 1994 through early 2003 working in the newspaper industry. As editor of a small town weekly known as the Benton Bulletin, he reported, photographed, editorialized, designed, laid out the pages and "took out the garbage and swept the floor" for four years.

After that newspaper shut its doors, the daily newspaper he competed against, Corvallis Gazette-Times, hired him as the cops and rural beat reporter. Later he covered environmental issues, filled in on the copy desk and served as interim city editor for eight months.

But the writer has done far more than write. Accepting Jesus Christ as his Lord and Savior as a 20-year-old in 1969, his experience as a Marine Corps tank mechanic took him from Los Angeles to the Oregon Coast where he wound up working in the timber industry as a logger, tree planter, fire fighter, mill hand and timber feller throughout Idaho, Washington, California and Oregon. It was after serious injuries as a logger and timber feller that he returned to college in 1991 to study journalism.

During his career in the timber industry, he also spent five years serving as a supervisor and principal in small Christian schools in both Oregon and Idaho. He now feels called to journal the workings of God in the early 21st Century.

Along with his wife, Bev, author of a small town monthly "nice" gossip column, he continues to live in their home a few miles outside the unincorporated town of Alsea, Oregon – also hometown for a daughter, son-in-law and grandson, and another son. Two other sons have moved from Alsea to Boise, Idaho where they and a daughter-in-law and three grandsons serve in the Church of the Harvest.

May 2002:

In the nation of Colombia, Alvaro Uribe gets elected as the new president of the nation. He comes to office with clear mandates from the citizenry to conquer the leftist guerillas, battle corruption within the government and revive a slumping economy. In the United States, missionary Gracia Burnham finally has time to reflect on her rescue from Philippine guerillas by government forces – a rescue that took the life of her husband, another kidnapped man and four guerillas.

Chapter 1: Shot, Beaten and Robbed

That day, May 27, 2002, had started so nice: good weather, good companionship and great goals. Now stripped naked and tied face down on the ground by the captors who were shoving a gun to his head and threatening to kill him, Ricardo Fuentes felt confident that his God could and would deliver him from the situation, but he had no guarantee.

Reeling from the pain of a 9 mm slug that crashed through the rear window of the 1994 Toyota pickup and lodged in his skull just behind one ear, not to mention the pain from the beating he and fellow traveler Marcos Jordan received in payment from the bandits for trying to evade the robbery, Fuentes could muster up one main thought. "So this is how my victims felt."

Fuentes grew up troubled, found trouble at a young age, dished it out and now found it once again coming back to him. But this was different, having since adopted the ways of his Savior. When he became a Christian, he left behind his old ways that led him to kill a man, flee his country and wind up in a California prison for armed robbery. Now he traveled with a mission from the Lord Jesus Christ.

But like his life, this trip was not turning out the way it started. Fuentes and Jordan had begun their journey from San Pedro Sula, Honduras, seven hours earlier, headed for Huehuetenango, Guatemala. Their job was to organize pastors and parishioners in Huehuetenango for an evangelistic crusade scheduled out about 12 months. World Wide Crusades, a small organization reaching out to Africa and Central America from a little Oregon Coast Range community called Alsea, would hold the crusade.

"It was a normal Monday for us, except the next day we needed to be in Huehuetenango," Fuentes recalls. To do that, he and Marcos Jordan would have to drive across a good stretch of Honduran road, in need of repair at best, and then traverse almost the entire east-west reach of Guatemala, nearly reaching Mexico. It would likely be a toss-up deciding which country's roads needed more improvement.

After weeks of planning for the journey, the two men intended to leave their homes around 11 a.m., but numerous delays set back the departure time. Both men are quite adapted to directing their vehicles through the chaotic traffic patterns that suggest that what lane markers do exist are painted on the streets and highways as mere suggestions, rather than driving dictates requiring obedience, so the heavy traffic with its black smoke-belching diesel trucks and buses didn't really create a tardy departure.

"We were late as usual. Brother Marcos is never on time, but we were ready to go anyway," says Fuentes lightheartedly.

Marcos Jordan tended to driving duties from San Pedro Sula to the Guatemalan border crossing, about a six-hour journey. With the sun shining down and the pickup running smoothly, the men talked easily about their families, religion, politics, ministries and other things to pass the time and help keep Jordan awake behind the wheel as he directed their pickup up and over passes and through winding valleys. Having worked together for World Wide Crusades over the past few years, they'd had their share of mishaps and near mishaps as they labored to prepare the way for crusades in Belize, Guatemala, El Salvador, Nicaragua and their own country of Honduras. But this day, it all looked good.

"Today we were happy, driving to a place where the Gospel needed to be preached," Fuentes said. "We were taking some U.S. dollars to finance an evangelistic crusade which would bring many souls to Jesus Christ."

Fuentes and Jordan have grown accustomed to the sometimes-chaotic scenes at border crossings in Central America. The cadre of shoe shiners, made up predominantly from little boys, blend their voices with those of the fast food vendors, moneychangers, beggars and anyone else with a product or service to sell, or need for cash. The crossing sites can become a teeming mass of humanity as travelers and drivers from buses, cars, pickups and commercial haulers work their way through long lines dealing with police and immigration officials, turning over more of their precious cash in order to get that final stamp of approval to continue their journeys into another country.

"All kinds of people are trying to sell you something. You see them, but the truth is that they are watching you – all your movements are controlled by somebody," says Fuentes.

After getting their passports checked and paying the toll to enter Guatemala, the men remembered that they only carried U.S. currency and the Honduran Lempiras – neither had the Guatemalan Quetzals they'd need to continue their journey, buy food and gas and pay for lodging. Knowing the danger that can come from revealing your cash on hand, the men looked around the area for a man they felt likely to be the most honest moneychanger at the border. With a quick exchange of cash, they stopped for fuel and more drinking water before heading off with the goal of making it to Guatemala City before dark.

Although Jordan had planned to stop in Guatemala City to avoid driving through unknown mountain roads after dark, something that can prove dangerous because of road conditions and desperate people willing to kill and steal, Fuentes planned to push on the extra six hours to make it to Huehuetenango for a 9 a.m. meeting on Tuesday with pastors.

Most Central American countries use periodic roadblocks to check for stolen vehicles entering their borders, as well as insure paperwork for drivers and vehicle are in order, and enforce the rule requiring drivers to wear a seat belt. That's why Fuentes paid little attention to a patrol car he noticed parked off the road about an hour later. He and Marcos checked to make sure their seat belts were on and Fuentes made sure he was driving the correct speed.

Passing by the patrol without drawing any particular notice, they thought there'd be no problem. Shortly after, though, the patrol car pulled onto the road and followed them for a few miles before telling them to pull over.

"I have been stopped before by these guys, but I've never experienced something like this. The first question was, 'Do you have any money on you?'" Fuentes said reflectively. "What kind of cops are these, we thought."

When they finished explaining who they were, their purpose for traveling in Guatemala and their destination, the police told Fuentes and Jordan to be careful because 10 miles outside Guatemala City where cars have to slow down on the highway, bandits were making the area dangerous.

"They told us that when the bandits get someone who's not carrying money, they get mad and kill them," Fuentes said. "We told them that we did not have any money, but it seems to me they did not believe us."

At the time, the two men thought the police were just trying to warn them and give them advice, but looking back on it now, they question that.

"I have a sense the police set us up, because when we went through the border, they stopped us and told us to be careful because of the dangers, but something was weird the way they asked us if we had money."

When Fuentes and Jordan were finally allowed to proceed, the journey once again looked as though it would remain a pleasant one.

"I remember we were counting the kilometers left to arrive in Guatemala City," recalls Jordan. "There was 41 left."

Marcos also remembers talking about where they would stop for rest once they got there. But the planned arrival soon met a sinister fate, one reflecting the breezy chill surrounding the approaching nightfall in the Guatemalan mountains.

The thoughts and discussion about the following day's agenda, adding to those of their approach to Guatemala City, sent the warnings and odd happenings at the border crossing about an hour before to the back of both men's minds.

But they came back like a bolt of lightning.

"All of a sudden a compact car was behind us," Fuentes explained. "The motor of this car had to be better than ours because it was coming up on us fast. The headlights were extremely strong so I decided to let them pass, but they didn't want to pass."

Quickly the warnings were resurrected.

"The first instance I knew they were bandits. They were yelling very suspiciously to us," Jordan said.

13

Fuentes agreed.

"Once they were window to window with our car, they yelled at us that they were police. From our experience and the way they were saying it, we knew they were not police. Marcos told me not to stop and I felt the same way, so I pushed them out of the road," Fuentes recalled. "At the moment they yelled at us to stop, they were pointing at me with a 9 mm gun, and they had a flashlight right in front of my face."

Despite the danger they knew they faced, Fuentes still managed to get a glimpse of five people in the compact car – two in front and three in back. His maneuver to run the bandits off the road looked as though it had worked.

"For a moment, we thought that was it," he said. "Something like that happened at El Salvador too, but this was not our lucky day. Just a few moments later they were chasing us again, and this time they were shooting at us. We fought to escape in our car, gun shots were all around, and we were panicked, thinking the worse was about to happen."

In the midst of battle or crisis, the detail of events often stand out distinctly different to each participant. The moments that followed Fuentes seeing a gun pointed his direction took on different meanings for Fuentes and Jordan.

When the 9 mm slug entered through the back window, it may have ricocheted around the pickup cab as Jordan remembers, or it may have simply made a direct hit just behind Fuentes' ear and stopped as if by the hand of God from killing him that instant. Doctors later confirmed that whether or not the slug first bounced around the cab before hitting him, Fuentes came within fractions of an inch from death.

Whatever path the bullet took, it's impact meant more trouble for the two men.

"I felt something cold in the back of my head, and it knocked me out for a few seconds," Fuentes said.

The few seconds when Fuentes lost consciousness seemed like a life-time to Marcos Jordan.

"He blacked out and fell down on top of my knees in my lap, and be-cause he was driving, I couldn't control it," Jordan explained. "I want-ed to accelerate, but his body was laying in a way keeping me from doing that. The car was in second, and I wanted to get it in third but couldn't do it. His body wouldn't allow me to control the gears so the car went into neutral. When I couldn't do anything, I took the steering wheel and pulled the car aside, trying to avoid hitting other cars going along the road."

As Fuentes came to, he saw that Jordan had his hands full trying to get his own seat belt loose, trying to help Fuentes undo his and at the same time telling him to try to keep driving. That did little good.

"The car got stuck," Fuentes explained. "I could not react properly, probably because I was wounded in the head."

Both men bolted from the car, crying in vain for help to passing-by motorists before running into the forest. Fuentes passed up one chance to get away. Bleeding and desperate, he almost jumped into the back of a truck passing through the chaotic scene, but he didn't know where Jordan was – at least for the moment.

Seconds later he turned to see that his friend had returned to the pickup where the bandits caught him as he tried to run into the forest. Fuentes too bolted for the woods, but to no avail.

"It was too late," said Fuentes simply. "They were really mad, point-ing their guns at us, kicking us in our chest and stomachs. They had all kinds of heavy guns."

After throwing them in the bed of the pickup, one man took the ban-dits' car and another drove the pickup. Two others took turns kicking Jordan and Fuentes in the back as they drove into the forest and out of sight from any help from the highway.

Stripped naked, hands tied behind their backs and thrown face first to the ground, Fuentes grew aware that his own blood oozed as a hot liquid over his head. He asked within himself, "Why is this happening to us, God?"

He didn't hear an answer from God. Instead, from the mist of memory came the vivid recollection of a similar experience – one where he was holding the gun.

In Los Angeles, California, Fuentes and a crime partner decided to rob someone at a bar. Finding just one man drinking at their chosen site, they waited for him to leave the bar. When he came out, Fuentes demanded his money, but the man had no cash. He had been buying his drinks with a credit card.

"I took him into the van and took all that he had, which was his clothes, his shoes, belt, shirt, everything," Fuentes recounted. "The only thing left was his trunks, his underwear. And I told him, 'Next time make sure you have money or it's going to be worse.'

"And I drop him on the freeway. That's one of the things I remembered when I was being robbed in Guatemala."

March 28, 1966:

One day earlier, B-52 bombers dropped bombs just one mile north of a Marine Corps unit engaged in combat near the DMZ in Vietnam. Gandhi and President Johnson began discussions on how to help India. Relationships between the United States and the Soviet Union were reportedly deteriorating. Don Drysdale and Sandy Koufax showed up for spring training with the Los Angeles Dodgers.

Chapter 2: Born and Set On a Rough Road

In a world filled with news of the war in Vietnam and growing opposition to the war, the birth of Ricardo Fuentes would appear as just another one of millions of others in third world nations and developed nations across the globe.

Honduras was edging closer to a brief but costly war in 1969 with El Salvador over borders and evicting thousands of illegal El Salvadorans living inside its borders. A year after Fuentes' birth, in the nation south of Honduras, Luis Somoza would die while serving as Nicaragua's leader. But even as opposition to the Somoza regime grew, mainly from the Sandinista National Liberation Front, Anastasio Somoza would become Nicaragua's president. To the north, civilian rule would be restored in Guatemala for the first time since the 1963 assassination of President Castillo.

When Fuentes was born on March 28, 1966, he arrived as the youngest of six children. Like many families in Central America, family life consisted of various forms of moneymaking ventures. His father, Catalino, was a rough man who ventured beyond coaxing beans, rice and other crops from a piece of leased farmland to delivering produce throughout Central America. Starting as an owner-operator of one truck, his outfit grew to include three trucks. That meant little time for family life. Add to that his penchant for strong drink, home rarely provided the feeling for his children that they had at least one place to feel safe and secure. Catalino would sometimes hit and kick his youngest son, leaving physical scars as well as the emotional ones. Those scars would later be added to by the cruelty of his brothers.

"Dad used to drink a lot, and he loved guns," Fuentes recalls. "He would get drunk coming from Nicaragua, El Salvador or Guatemala. He didn't like us to make much noise – we were afraid even to talk. He'd yell, 'Shut up!' My sisters, my brothers, everyone, we were all afraid. He didn't give us a hug or kiss or anything like that, showing us the love he had. We were raised without love in our house. ... He provided, but he was never at home."

The life Fuentes observed in his family collided with any views of God he'd received from the same family that had all been baptized into the Catholic religion. Despite the contradictions Fuentes observed, the Catholicism he knew and rejected would later make it difficult for him to turn his life over to Jesus Christ's call upon him.

The one area of stability Fuentes and his siblings did find came from their mom, Amparo. Using her talent for tailoring, Amparo worked out of her home off a narrow street where patrons could come to be fitted for clothes. That same spot would later serve as a sort of home-cooked fast-food restaurant. Like many homes and businesses along the alley-like streets of many San Pedro Sula areas, iron works, some decorative and some reminiscent of jail bars, kept customers and thieves from the work area when business hours were over. Fuentes remembers as early as 11 years old working on the sewing machines his mother owned.

When it came time to take care of the calls coming from school directors or teachers, Amparo dealt with the situation.

Such a life left a few good memories, but not many. Although he can still remember the pleasant scent of oranges from the produce his father hauled, growing up around older brothers who were as unsupervised as he was left its own mark, a long-lasting one. But Fuentes grew very close, and remains so today, with his next older sister, Josefa.

"We were just both alone," Josefa recalls. "I gave him orders what to do, to eat this and do that. And he told me, 'When I grow up, you won't give me any orders.'"

Josefa now pastors a church just across the street from the home where she, Fuentes and the rest of the family grew up. With his brothers being four and seven years older, Fuentes rarely got included in the occasional soccer games they found time for with friends and neighbors.

The cruelty that can grow toward fellow siblings when unchecked by supervision escalated to the point of creating deep hatred. While his dad's truck sat idle, it sometimes became a wonderful playground for such games as hide-and-seek. Inside the truck, however, at times also became a torture chamber of sorts. Once while spending the night sleeping in the truck at the age of 8 or 9, the abuse grew so bad that Fuentes purposed in his heart to one day kill one of his brothers. Had it not been for their mother, that purpose might have been fulfilled. Four years later, after the boiling point had long since been reached, the young teen-aged Fuentes took after his brother with one of his father's rifles. While he would have willingly dispatched the life of his brother, he could not shoot his mother who stood between him and his tormentor.

"I was violent all my life," Fuentes says. "I hated them and was always looking for revenge for what they did to me."

By the time he reached 12, and without a steady presence of his father for he and the rest of the family, Fuentes says he grew rebellious and hated everyone, even himself. But most of his resentment he kept in reserve for his father.

"I was angry at him and wanted to pay him back," he said. "When I needed him, he didn't care about me. I was angry with my relatives, with God and everyone."

Other family members handled the developments in their lives similarly. One brother and one sister would run away from the family, making their way to the United States long before Fuentes made the trek. Little did they know that they too would end up playing a part in God's plan for the family.

"At about 12, I started thinking about making my own way in life. I wasn't very successful," says Fuentes as he reflects on his past.

His early decisions included starting to drink and run with loose girls. By the time he'd reached 13, he was smoking marijuana.

Fuentes managed to finish elementary school and move on to high school, where he quickly became popular, as well as proved to be a good athlete and a quick fighter. But all that time, the hatred toward his father and brothers continued boiling within the cauldron of his heart. In efforts to lash out, he became even more rebellious and ungrateful toward his parents. When they'd give him money for schoolbooks, he'd spend it on alcohol.

At 14, he fell in love with Doris, a 13-year-old girl, and began a sexual relationship with her. He sought to have her live with him at his parents' home, something not that unusual in nations such as Honduras, but his parents not only objected to the idea, they objected to the girl. She couldn't cook, wash clothes or do many of things women have to do to take care of their husbands, they said.

"She was a beautiful girl, and I felt I was in love for the first time,"

Fuentes recalls. "I felt like she was the only woman in my life."

As father and head of the home, Catalino would later change his mind, at least for a while. About a year later she moved into his room, which was isolated from the rest of the home.

"At that age I remember being in love. Dad didn't like her very much and told me to let her go," Fuentes said.

As a result, the young couple decided suicide was their only answer. Gleaning an idea from a Mexican movie they'd watched, they each drank a jar of insecticide.

When one of Fuentes' aunts heard the noises that came with the impending death caused by chemicals, she found them and discovered what they had done ... almost too late. Once she saw how close they were to death, she rushed them to the hospital where emergency staff saved their lives by pumping the deadly fluid from their stomachs.

"I was babbling and this white stinking stuff came out of my mouth. My eyes were already white – I was dying," Fuentes said.

The combination of quick medical work and prescribed medicines managed to save both their lives, and despite all the chaos it created, the suicide attempt failed to accomplish their goals.

"The funny thing was, they didn't allow me to live with her so I had to leave her anyway."

Just how deeply in love the young lady was with Fuentes showed itself shortly after their attempted suicide when she lost interest in him and started spending time with another man.

While recovering in the hospital, "Something weird happened," Fuentes recalls. A male nurse came to talk him about his need to accept the salvation of God through believing that the blood Jesus Christ shed on the cross had already paid the price for the forgiveness he needed from God for his sin.

"He said, 'Young man, why do you want to kill yourself? Don't you know that Jesus loves you?' I told him I was a Catholic, and that seemed to be good enough," Fuentes said. "I told my sins to a priest and that was good enough.

"I didn't know anything about Jesus except what I was taught in the Catholic Church. I knew that Jesus was a man nailed to a cross, but the Jesus he was talking about was the one who saved my life even when I didn't know him."

That thought stood in stark contrast to all he had learned about Jesus.

"The Catholic Church taught me about a man who died on the cross," he remembers. "He had no power. He had eyes but couldn't see, ears but he couldn't hear ... a mouth and he was full of love, but he could do nothing for me when my brothers abused me when I was young."

All he knew was that he wanted to run to his girl friend's hospital room and be with her. Now, he finds it interesting that he couldn't wait to be with her, and yet she was helping take him toward death.

The attempted suicide left Fuentes battling tuberculosis for nearly three years. The insecticide had hardened portions of his lungs, leaving him to spit blood frequently over the next two and a half years. It also left him growing angrier over his lot in life.

"I was so angry I went to discotheques, prostitutes, used drugs and alcohol, trying to find escape from my life," he says. "Nobody loved me and no one wanted me to be happy. The doctors said if I kept living like this I would die, which is exactly what I wanted to do.

"I didn't understand then that God had a plan for my life."

Along his teenage road of life, somehow Fuentes learned to dance quite well. Despite still recovering from the effects of the insecticide he drank in the attempt to kill himself, he danced well enough to attract the attention of one young lady. As Fuentes' wife and mother of their two teenaged daughters, Juanita still remembers the early 1980s when she met him.

"I liked it that he took me dancing, and I loved to dance," she reflected. "He was a good dancer."

Fuentes had a different view.

"This girl's saying she loves me, and I didn't love her. I just wanted sex, to satisfy my flesh," he says.

As boyfriend and girlfriend, neither of them knew or served the Lord Jesus Christ. At 17, Fuentes was already an alcoholic. Juanita, 21 at the time, seemed to look beyond the alcoholism, at least for a while, to see something her man could become. They started living together, and she met full approval of his parents.

Neither of them were concerned about the possibility of becoming parents because doctors had told Juanita she had the birth organs of an infant and bearing children would not be a part of her life.

God says in the New Testament book of First Corinthians that He has chosen the foolish things of the world to confound the wise, the weak things of the world to confound the mighty things and the base, cowardly and things of low estate to bring to nothing the wisdom and ways of the world, in order to keep us from glorifying ourselves in His presence.

Three years later, on December 4, 1985, their first-born daughter entered the world – the same year Fuentes turned 19 and graduated from school.

"Lucy is a miracle baby. ... I considered her a graduation gift," Fuentes exclaimed. "When we met, I knew Juanita was barren or had problems, and I was sick too. We just accepted each other the way we were."

Although he could accept Juanita for who she was, he found plenty of things in life he couldn't accept, which allowed him to point the blame for his state of affairs on others. That's what briefly drew him to the Communist Party in Honduras during the wars in El Salvador and Nicaragua. At the time, he liked what he understood of the communistic philosophies of Marx, Lenin and Engels.

"The communists offered much to the poor. I liked that," he says. But it's hard to live with universal ideals while the main goal of day-to-day living is finding another drink of liquor to dull the pain inside the soul. He left behind his friends involved with the political party and thinks that it probably saved his life. As far as he knows, most or all of those friends are already dead.

Two years after Lucy entered the world, the birth of Kimberly added to Fuentes' growing family responsibilities.

Isaiah the prophet said in the Old Testament that one day the wolf also shall live with the lamb, and the leopard shall lie down with the kid; and the calf and the young lion and the yearling together; and a little child shall lead them.

Sometimes, even now, God uses the children to reach entire families and draw them to Him. For Ricardo Fuentes and Juanita, the birth of their children would eventually lead both of them and many family members to the Savior's feet. But that path would take Juanita through a lot of pain and agony.

Fuentes admits that he was unfaithful to Juanita many times, including her times of pregnancy. He spent his time gambling away his money and getting so drunk that some nights he would end up sleeping in the gutter.

"I was unfaithful to her many times, and she knew it, but I didn't care," he said. "We lived that way for nine years."

Juanita herself recalls that she too had her own bouts of playing with infidelity, delighting in attracting the attention of married men. But her love for Fuentes continued to amaze him.

"I even spent her paycheck on drugs and alcohol, and she was always waiting for me," he recalls. "Sometimes she would cry and say, 'Why do you get so drunk?' and 'Why do you hurt me?'"

During all that time, getting in fights became a normal part of Fuentes' life. As one of four men who were "protecting their neighborhood," he and a quasi gang didn't rob or kill anyone. The "only" drug they used was marijuana.

"We ruled, but we didn't consider ourselves a gang," Fuentes said. "We just fought for our girls. ... No one touched our girls."

In 1986 the group broke up, with two making it to the United States, another being killed in his native El Salvador and Fuentes being left to deal with his own mess.

As a new and growing Christian, and Fuentes' closest sister, Josefa started taking the couple's children to church. Persistence on her part paid off, and Juanita finally consented to attend church with her. At some point, she too accepted the Lord's salvation through the shed blood of Jesus Christ. Although having experienced the rebirth that Christians talk about, Juanita still had some struggles of her own to face. She'd grown used to going places with Fuentes where they could drink and dance.

"He was not taking me there anymore," she said.

Wanting to serve and obey God, she started praying that Fuentes too would come to serve the Lord. That created a new set of frustrations.

"I felt like the Lord wasn't listening to my prayers," she said. "I was asking Him to change him my way, and he was doing it differently. I was kind of angry. Instead of things improving, it was getting worse."

And so it would continue that way for years to come.

President Ronald Reagan and Mikhail Gorbachev, leader of the Soviet Union, met several times and finally signed a treaty to reduce the number of nuclear arms each country would hold. Palestinians in the West Bank and Gaza Strip began an uprising against Israel's military rule of those territories.

Chapter 3: Someone Had to Die

The first chapter of the Old Testament book of Proverbs looks like a road map for the choices Fuentes would follow in the years after his nineteenth birthday, graduation from school and the birth of his and Juanita's first daughter.

Wisdom cries without; she utters her voice in the streets: She cries in the chief place of concourse, in the openings of the gates: in the city she utters her words, saying, "How long, you simple ones, will you love simplicity? and the scorners delight in their scorning, and fools hate knowledge? Turn you at my reproof: behold, I will pour out my spirit unto you, I will make known my words unto you.

"Because I have called, and you refused; I have stretched out my hand, and no man regarded; but you have set at nought all my counsel, and would none of my reproof: I also will laugh at your calamity; I will mock when your fear comes; when your fear comes as desolation, and your destruction comes as a whirlwind; when distress and anguish comes upon you."

Then shall they call upon me, but I will not answer; they shall seek me early, but they shall not find me: for that they hated knowledge, and did not choose the fear of the Lord: they would none of my counsel: they despised all my reproof. Therefore

shall they eat of the fruit of their own way, and be filled with their own devices.
(KJV)

Time and again he would continue to make the wrong choices, casting aside council from the Word of God, parents, and the mother of his two children. Though those choices really just grew from those he made as a child, the anger and desire for revenge cultivated as a child grew right along his wrong choices, resulting in drastic consequences. Like the poppy flower waiting for the sun's heat to open its pedals, Fuentes' anger just waited for the right conditions to boil out from the vessel holding it in.

Although he no longer took Juanita dancing and drinking with him, in part because of her becoming a Christian and in part because she had children to stay home with, Fuentes found plenty of time himself to go drinking and carousing.

Life sank so low for him that he and one of his fellow revelers decided to rob one of the Catholic churches. They came away empty handed and disappointed when they didn't find anything to steal. His alcoholism continued to destroy his life while Juanita's life took a different turn.

"She started going to church, but I didn't want anything to do with church," Fuentes says. "I refused to go. She tried everything."
Instead, he continued his downhill roll. When his mother closed her tailor shop, Fuentes lost his source of employment. He had made an earlier escape from the abuse he found at home by attending college, where he received training as an accountant during what he would later refer to as the happiest years of his life. That schooling soon helped him land a job as an accountant. But the job turned out to be another short-term stop for him. Just months after he was hired, he was fired for embezzling. For now, only the help of his sister kept him from

spending a long time looking out on the world from behind bars. She provided the money to pay back the employer and pay the fine to get him out of jail.

With the landing of another blow to his self-esteem and his ability to reach all that he seemed to be grasping for, he started drinking even more. The continual drunkenness and late-night habits created such a feeling of despair within the home that Juanita moved out and took the children with her.

In 1987 he tried twice to make it to the United States. The first time he was arrested as an illegal alien in Mexico and spent time in the Guaymas jail where prisoners reportedly are packed thirty to a cell and fed one piece of bread and one cup of coffee each day. The bathroom facilities consisted of a hole in the floor.

After seven days in Guaymas, authorities sent him to the federal immigration jail in Mexico City where he spent three days before being taken to Guatemala.

Not a quick learner in his alcohol dependent state of mind, as soon as he returned to San Pedro Sula, he sold his refrigerator, television and radio to finance a second attempt. That money went almost as fast as he got his hands on it.

"I spent the money on booze and girls, and we didn't really try. When the money was gone, we came back."

With no money, no job and no hope, Fuentes and Juanita separated for more than a year. While she landed a good paying job, he continued the downward spiral.

"I was a hopeless drunk – depressed, angry, frustrated, and I just wanted to fight," he said.

One night in a bar, he saw himself for what he was: a bum in dirty clothing, begging for drinks and sleeping at the bar. In that moment, he thought he'd change. After slamming his glass to the bar and breaking it, he announced, "That's enough!" and moved away from the bar.

But resolve doesn't always provide the power needed to complete such a change in life. After returning to his parents' house and asking for help, his determination melted away like ice in the sun. He lost a job at a supermarket because of his drinking, and that probably kept him for being arrested again for the stealing he was doing from the market.

He finally landed a job he was able to keep for two years – teaching English – but even there he stole from his boss.

With Lucy now six years old and Kimberly four, Juanita sent them as ambassadors in an attempt to put the relationship back together.

"Juanita was going to church, but she was very different now," Fuentes said. "She never nagged me."

Although God had made great changes in her life, she still had more to go, and the Master has a way of showing where those changes are needed.

In December 1989, she returned to Fuentes' home, only to find him dressed in new clothes and sporting a new girlfriend. That encounter led to a fist fight.

"Juanita hit her real bad," he said. "She came back, my girlfriend left, but I didn't stop seeing her."

Need really prompted the reunion, with Juanita now battling cancer and Fuentes feeling obliged to repay the kindness she'd shown him when he was sick with TB. The arrangement worked for a while, but she still wanted him to go to church with her. The tension grew so great that she eventually said he had to attend church with her or she would leave with the children again. He conceded, and they attended an evangelical style of church. That didn't set well with him.

"I didn't like it. I didn't like the clapping and singing, and I made fun of the worship and mocked it. I saw everyone happy, and I hated them," he explained. "I was too tough for this church stuff. I left in the middle of the service and went to the bar until the service was over."

He had told Juanita that one reason he didn't want to go to church was because all the people there really just wanted his money. With such a view, it didn't surprise him to see the pastor stop by his work place.

"He came to visit me at work, and I say, 'See, now they want to steal my paycheck,'" he remembers with a smile.

But Fuentes didn't realize how close he was coming to paying a heavy price for his drunken brawling and refusal to humble himself before God and receive the power required to make the changes he desperately needed to make.

At another Friday night service later on, he reluctantly "accepted the Lord", but says he didn't mean it and just did it to please Juanita. Truly, after the service he returned to the pattern that had controlled his life for years.

"She went to the house, and I went to the bar."

That night after leaving the bar, it started raining hard. Drunk, wet, hungry and angry, he got to the house and asked Juanita to fix dinner.

"She said, "Get out of here, I don't want to see you anymore.'"

Stumbling his way to the kitchen area and drunkenly struggling to open the lock on the door, he declared flatly that Juanita could not be a Christian like she said she was because she wouldn't get up and fix him something to eat.

When he finally got into the kitchen, he turned the light switch on and off repeatedly, but to no avail. Mad and getting angrier, Fuentes shouted, "There is no God and there is no devil either. If God really exists, someone is going to kill me or I'm going to kill someone. And as proof, that light will turn on by itself.

"It did, and I was scared. I started crying and trembling because I knew what I had done. ... I had insulted God."

That scare not only sobered him up, but it sent him hurrying to Juanita's room, begging her to pray for him because someone was surely going to kill him. She prayed and told him not to worry because the Lord would take care of him.

"I felt better, went to bed and woke up the next day like nothing had happened."

But one thing Fuentes continued to show, he remained a slow learner when it came the concept of cause and effect. The following Friday night he again attended church with Juanita and again returned to the bar after the service. His words uttered a week before would return to haunt him that night and for years to come.

After spending some time drinking with a friend, he grew hungry and suggested they go look for some cooked chicken to buy. Although the many small eateries lining the narrow streets throughout neighborhoods of San Pedro Sula generally make it easy to find something to eat, the late hour of their search made it nearly fruitless and instead led to disaster.

They found one vendor, but she had no chicken. His friend, however, saw one of his friends eating the last piece of chicken, and as a prank went to him, took the piece of chicken and ate it.

"That man got mad so the lady called her husband, telling him that two drunk men were creating problems at her business," Fuentes recalls. "This man came and didn't argue with no one. He came directly at me and started fighting with me because he thought I was the one causing trouble. ... I was drunk, and I had a knife."

"He was very big and well built," Fuentes continued. "He didn't count on me having a knife in my belt. He tried to hit me twice ... I didn't think so very well because I was drunk, so I took the knife out of my belt and stuck him, just once, but it was enough ... just once, but it was my bad luck – he died. He dropped to the floor. I saw him in the dirt begging for help and I started running. He had tried to kill me, but I was faster."

Although he wouldn't know it for a while, two hours later the man would die, but Fuentes had already started a new life, one where he would be running from the law.

And run he did, but only to a deeper and darker abyss.

January 1993:

Bill Clinton began his first term as President of the United States. He appointed Janet Reno to serve as the U.S. Attorney General, the first woman to hold the post. The same year, Nelson Mandela, president of the African National Congress since 1991, and then-President F. W. de Klerk of South Africa won the Nobel Peace Prize for their work to end apartheid, thus enabling the country's nonwhites to participate in the South African government.

Chapter 4: A Long Way to Run

Driving past the small cantina where Ricardo Fuentes killed a man ten years ago, it seems oddly quiet. Now, the blue and white paint from the building's Pepsi advertising paint job has started peeling away, particularly at the doorway covered by a slightly tattered white cloth, the same kind that flutters in the breeze from the one open window.

Located on a street much wider than the alley-like surroundings where Fuentes grew up, this building sports a corrugated tin awning that stretches out from the cantina to cover the sidewalk, something not seen on many buildings in the vicinity. But like the door to el baño (the bathroom) several feet from the entrance to the cantina, the awning too shows the aging affect of the hot Central American sun in the decade since the killing.

From that site, still holding the bloody knife that didn't even belong to him, Fuentes stumbled out into a brand new world, a scary one full of uncertainty.

"Now, I was a killer on the run."

If caught by police, he knew he'd go to prison. Under Honduran law for most citizens, when someone is killed, someone else is going to prison, even if it is in an act of self-defense as Fuentes saw his case.

But prison was only one alternative. If the victim's family caught up with him first, they would kill him.

Juanita remembers him returning far earlier than usual that night. He also passed by his usual request for something to eat, telling her he'd go eat at a friend's house. It wasn't until the next morning that she heard from others about the knifing.

Now nearly 20 and attending college away from home, daughter Lucy still remembers the night her dad went away. He had caught a bus to the mountain town of Copan, close to the Mayan ruins and the Guatemalan border – where his father had a house, as well as where Juanita's mother lived.

"I just remember it was at night and everybody was sighing and giving hugs to my dad," she recalls. "I thought he was leaving, but the next day I would see him again in the morning."

It took her some time before she realized he would be gone for a long time, maybe forever. She also remembers receiving the tambourine he sent her after he left Honduras.

Going to church took on a new meaning for the family left behind.

"We attended church and my mom was telling us to pray for Dad, and I was praying," she said.

Fuentes had been running from the law and keeping his head low to avoid being seen by family members of the dead man for about six weeks when he set out from Copan in January 1993. His oldest brother tried to talk him into surrendering to the police, saying that now he had to pay for what he'd done or run all his life. He'd have no part of turning himself in, choosing rather to run.

Many Hondurans try to make it illegally to the United States, according to Fuentes, and although he failed twice before, this time had to be different. The years of alcohol hadn't dulled his desire to stay alive and stay out of prison.

"I had to get to the States one way or another," he said.

That meant just one thing for Fuentes and his family – scraping together enough money to hire someone to get him there. Commonly called coyotes, they're hired to help would-be illegals make it past the pitfalls, check points and border patrols while traveling from their home country to the United States. Some may be part of a larger organization and be better equipped, or like the one Fuentes hired, just a poor man trying to make a living. Likewise, some coyotes attempt to deal honestly with their clients, and others, as has been reported in the news media, treat their clients like so much chattel, willing to abandon them to death in overcrowded railroad boxcars and freight trucks.

For Fuentes, it also meant putting aside all the fears about the journey. Having attempted it twice already, Fuentes had heard plenty of stories about bandits who assault and rob illegal immigrants trying to make their way to the States. Some are even killed.

"I feared being caught by those guys," he said.

He met the coyote at the Honduran-Guatemalan border, and traveling by buses, the pair enjoyed an uneventful trip across Guatemala. Reaching the border crossing into Mexico meant abandoning the highway.

While an increasing number of tourists now travel to parts of the Naranjo River to enjoy whitewater rafting, for Fuentes and his coyote, it meant waiting for a canoe to take them across the river so they could slip past the border crossing and authorities.

After crossing the river by night, they made their way to Mexico City by taxis and by riding in the back of trucks. Once they reached the capital, Fuentes had to make a call to the States.

"I called my sister to send me more money because the coyote said we'd run out of money. I don't know how because he didn't spend that much, but that was his job," he explained.

Once they got the money, they pushed on for the city of Queretaro. They caught another ride in a truck, but a federal check point on the road forced them to not only spend a night trudging through the desert, but also to put even more trust in the truck driver. The checkpoints are set up throughout the region with the specific goal of snaring illegal aliens and sending them back to their legal country. That was something Fuentes would do whatever was necessary to avoid.

"The truck driver told us there was a check point a mile ahead and that we should spend the night in the desert, and he would meet us in another place. That was quite an experience. We were chased by some animals – I don't know what, maybe wolves."

After spending a night without sleep while running and seeking some place to hide from whatever was chasing them, finding the truck driver waiting for them where he said he'd be came as welcome relief. Although it got them past one more obstacle to reaching the States, it didn't get Fuentes past a new battle beginning to struggle for a foothold within his mind.

When he heard that the man he stabbed had died, initially he felt no real remorse, in part because he believed it was an act of self-defense. But that stance did little to ease his conscience or subconscious thoughts.

"I had nightmares every night, killing him one time and another and another. I had dreams every night and every night, in them he came to fight against me," he explained. "I had to stop him every time."

An uneventful ride in the truck to Chihuahua came as a welcome relief to Fuentes, despite his nightly battles with the past. After parting company with the truck driver, the two men caught a bus bound for Tijuana, just miles from the line Fuentes so desired to cross. Once arriving at the border town where millions of tourists cross out of and back into California each year, the coyote again called Fuentes' family, telling them they needed to send more money for the $300 a head price tag they'd have to pay to be transported from San Ysidro to Los Angeles – if they made it across the border without being caught.

Fuentes doesn't know if the border patrol has changed any of its practices by now, but at that time almost the entire patrol ended one shift just before midnight. That left about a 15-minute window of time for illegals to make a dash across the border while one shift went off duty and one came on.

To get ready for the sprint, Fuentes and the coyote covered their shoes and pants with plastic bags so that if they were stopped on the other side, wet pants and shoes wouldn't give away the fact that they'd just made the border dash.

With the darkness of night blurring the lines of distinction between one shape and another, the two men were soon surprised to see just how many others had likewise been using the cover of darkness, waiting for the shift change.

"They all knew they have 15 minutes. When we started running, we saw all kinds of people running on the beach and in the river," Fuentes said. "There were so many, and it was just one old policeman trying to stop all of us – He couldn't get anyone."

Once across the border, Fuentes, the coyote and some others climbed over a fence to the San Ysidro Freeway where the awaiting van whisked them off to Los Angeles. Ham and cheese sandwiches eaten in the van probably have never tasted better for the passengers on their way to Los Angeles.

"I was so worried, I didn't have a choice because jail was waiting for me," Fuentes said. "Also, my family told me some people were looking for me to kill me: at my job, my house, all the places I used to be."

He had made it, safe now from the past, except for what he would soon discover he brought with him.

In the country of South Africa, the first truly open elections in the nation's history were held, allowing all races to vote. Nelson Mandela was elected president and the majority of seats in the National Assembly went to members of the African National Congress. In Texas, a new baseball stadium opened for the Texas Rangers, owned in part by then Texas Governor George W. Bush.

Chapter 5: Betrayed and Arrested

After getting in trouble with his grandfather, who served as the pastor of a small rural church, a boy about four years old expressed more wisdom than adults sometimes display. He said, "The problem is Papa, no matter where I go, there I am."

That's a piece of advice Fuentes could have used after reaching the United States. A brief upward climb from his historic downward spiral marked his life shortly after arriving, but that would soon be eclipsed by the trouble the illegal alien now living in the Land of the Free would find. That trouble came from the same sources he'd cultivated in his native Honduras.

"In Honduras I make a deal with God," Fuentes recalls. "If you exist, let me escape this place and I will serve you. I believe he allowed me to go to the U.S., but I didn't keep my part of the deal."

He made other promises too, which he at least tried to fulfill early in his life in the States.

One of those promises was to Juanita, that he would send money to support her and their two daughters. One day after his Sunday arrival, he started to work helping lay carpet. His employer had promised to pay him $45 a day, but at week's end, he gave Fuentes just $150, saying that he hadn't yet been paid for the job. Despite that disappointment, Fuentes sent $90 home and kept the rest to buy a little food and some beer.

Trying his best to keep his promises, he also called Juanita to let her know he'd arrived safely. Word of his safety and news of money soon reaching her lifted her sagging spirits.

"She was so happy," Fuentes recalls.

Indeed, Juanita remembers well the early days of her lover's life in the United States.

"At the beginning there was a lot of communication," she said. "Every week he'd call and send money. But after that, he didn't call, and he sent no money."

During that time, she says her faith in God continued to grow, but so did her need to work harder to earn money to support her daughters. Help came from Fuentes' parents, who willingly took in Juanita and the girls as their own, allowing them to continue living in their home.

"The day he fled, I got on my knees, and I raised my hands to heaven and put him in the hands of the Lord," Fuentes' mother, Amparo, recalls. "And God gave me the desires of my heart, and I felt thankful to God.

"The place for Juanita with the two little girls was with me, and from that moment on, the Lord gave me strength. His wife and daughters did not get away from my side, and we shared a lot of very sad moments for the next seven years."

Back in California, Fuentes found that the fear that forced him to flee his home country came along with him. Fearing that family members of the man he killed would chase him down in the States and kill him, he bought a shotgun. By this time the fear had grown so deep that he slept with his arms around the weapon every night.

Fuentes' promise to God to serve Him if He would allow him to escape soon rang hollow.

After two weeks on the job as a carpet layer, the opportunity to work as a cook for $4.25 an hour seemed like a good idea. But the job had one drawback – working just six hours on four days each week. That wasn't enough for Fuentes.

When he met a man from Mexico who sold strawberries all around California, the two teamed up ... for better and worse.

Work wise, things went well, as Fuentes seemed to have a natural talent for salesmanship. Although he'd later face time behind bars for far more serious crimes, he had his first scrape with the law in California during that time – for selling strawberries in the street.

"That's illegal too," Fuentes recalls with a smile.

His ability to sell strawberries provided him plenty of money, too much in fact, considering the character of his boss.

In the Old Testament book of Proverbs, Chapter 22, we're warned, *"Make no friendship with an angry man, and with a furious man do not go, lest you learn his ways and set a snare for your soul."* Chapter 29 continues that line of thought. *"An angry man stirs up strife, and a furious man abounds in transgression."* (NKJV)

That's more advice Fuentes could have used.

"It was good money, but this friend was violent and drank a lot ... every day, all day long," he remembers.

According to Fuentes, Hondurans have a saying that a child whimpers and the mother hits him, meaning that when someone has a bad habit, no one can stop it.

And so it came to pass that Fuentes would join in the drinking, fighting, and suffering consequences for the messes he continued to make.

"I became an alcoholic again ... the same spot, drinking every day," he said. "Everything I'd done in Honduras I was doing again. I had a shotgun at my house and didn't trust anyone."

Returning to that old downward spiral brought only a few fights with some of the Mexican in the area, and he considered them not too serious. But true to form, he also returned to making more poor decisions, and almost as if designed by an enemy, to encounters with people who would encourage his predisposition to fall.

While in the city of Lynwood, he met a fellow Honduran, reportedly the leader of a gang. After introducing him to the gang, Fuentes was accepted as a member, passing through the gang's ritual initiation. Although he really didn't understand what gang life would mean, the move fed two of his needs – security and protection from the fear of being on his own as an illegal alien, and at the same time, a desire to show off his own belief in his power.

"I forgot about God," Fuentes says reflectively. "I thought I was invincible."

But not too invincible. He kept his gang association secret from his sister because she told him shortly after he arrived in the States that if he got involved in a gang, she'd make him leave the home he had at her house. Having been a Christian for about twenty years, she tried to talk to her brother about his need for Jesus Christ, but those conversations with her brother continued to fall on deaf ears.

Fuentes soon found out what gang life with this particularly violent gang was all about. Although selling drugs took the lead role in activity, fighting with other gangs and beating up on individuals came with the package ... so too did the sexual favors for which some girls and women would trade for the coveted drugs the gang members had access to.

The gang's territory included parts of Watts, Lynwood and Huntington Park. Selling drugs in the territory centered a lot around the "hot corner" of State Street and Sequoia. Part of the drug-selling scene also required them to cut cocaine with Tylenol or baking soda, as well as produce crack cocaine. As boss, the gang leader, Danny, kept all the profits, something that bothered Fuentes.

"I wanted my own gang," he said.

To his benefit, that was one desire that never got fulfilled.

Although the steady diet of drugs, alcohol, women and card playing appealed to him in some ways, after about three months, the violence got to him. One night Danny took Fuentes to the city of Compton where they ended up beating a black man with a baseball bat.

The type of violence and fighting the gang continually handled, sometimes even involving guns, as well as the steady round of drug selling, convinced Fuentes he needed to get out of that situation, and it could even take something drastic to make it happen. As a new member to the gang, he had two things going for him that could help him achieve that goal. He had not yet been tattooed with the gang's emblem, and for some reason, they seemed to respect a gang member who turns his life over to Christ.

In an odd assessment from a man running from Honduran police and blood feuding relatives of the victim of his borrowed knife blade, and yet continuing to live in the drunken state in which the killing occurred, Fuentes realized he wanted out of the gang.

"I was a little afraid of all the fighting, and they had guns and I didn't want to be shot," Fuentes recalls. "I had problems in Honduras and didn't want them here."

After telling Danny and the others that he had become a Christian and could no longer participate in the gang activities, they let him go. To make it look good, Fuentes did return to the habit of attending church services.

"I did for a while, and was reconciled to the Lord," he says. "And things started going good for me and my family."

That reconciliation again caused him to stop his habitual drinking – at least temporarily. After nearly six months of living a life totally opposed to anything he'd known in the past, a new desire crept into his life, one that would ultimately lead him back to that same old familiar path. Living so far from Juanita and their girls for 16 months or so, the thought of remaining faithful to his family butted against his desire for female companionship.

As though riding a water slide to an awaiting pool of worldly pleasure, Fuentes found that his involvement with another woman led him quickly back to drinking, drugs and selling drugs.

This time, the sister who had watched over him since he arrived had had enough of her brother's life style.

"I backslid from church," he explained simply. "Now I became a wino, and my sister threw me away from her house and said she didn't want to see me."

Still having money in his pockets, he rented a room at a hotel. But even that security felt threatened as his once again steady drunkenness led to losing his job, loosing his car, and as he simply describes it, "Everything." He got caught shoplifting a package of Tylenol and spent two nights in jail. After release from jail, he later found himself so hungry that he went looking through garbage cans for something to eat. He says he distinctly remembers the night he found a piece of pizza in a box, looked at it and then ate it.

Once again, he had to admit he was not doing too well at living his own life.

In an attempt to keep his $30 a day motel room, Fuentes invited two Mexican friends to come and live with him and share the rent. At $10 each, the men could probably afford to continue with the degraded life style each one seemed to be chasing.

"It was a mess – drinking, playing cards, drugs, dating whores, the evil life again," Fuentes said.

With none of them having jobs, they still had to find a way to support themselves – a nearly certain recipe for robbery and shoplifting. Fuentes finds it interesting that he remembers the time they spent stealing from others as actually cutting into the time they had for getting drunk.

Using loose, bulky shirts, the men would go to places such as liquor stores and steal beer and wine. Sometimes they'd even remember they needed to steal some food to eat.

"We shoplifted everything, and somehow we never got caught. It's amazing," Fuentes says reflectively.

Somehow, with all the shoplifting and robbery, he managed to keep a supply of drugs around. Paying for those was a priority.

"I paid for my drugs," he says. "I didn't pay my rent, but I paid my drugs."

With his penchant for going from bad to worse, the time soon came that would push him down at least one more wrung of his downward spiraling ladder. And the action of the past that sent him fleeing from Honduras would again raise its ugly head.

Drinking and playing cards in his crowded motel room one night in April 1994, Fuentes pulled out of the game in order to let another Mexican man play while he went to his room to relax. When he left, no one seemed to be having problems getting along, but soon he heard a Honduran friend call out his nickname, "Bato," which means "I beat." He told Fuentes that the Mexican was tricking him and stealing his money, not wanting to pay up when he lost.

"I went to him and told him that if you don't pay my buddy, I will hit you and him too," Fuentes said. "I had a little knife and stabbed him six times. He survived, and I didn't go to jail because he was an illegal too and didn't report it. He couldn't report it because he was a thief. I knew it. He was my partner."

But his stabbed crime partner created his own ways to get even, and he deeply wanted his revenge. The following week he called the drunken Fuentes and invited him to help him and another man rob a gas station. They needed transportation and Fuentes now had a car.

"I said not today, but I have my gun and my Buick, so they convinced me," he recalls. "He talked with the other Mexican before I got there, and they decided to set me up."

Fuentes drove the Buick to a gas station in Orange County and got out to rob the station. When he threatened to kill the woman, she cowered on the floor behind the desk and told him to take it all. Returning outside to find his car and accomplices gone, he realized he'd been set up.

"For a miserable $100," he exclaims. "And my partner called the police and said there was a gas station being robbed ... my own partner. We've slept with the same woman, ate from the same plate, ran from the same buildings."

Fuentes walked away still in a drunken stupor, trying to put together some sort of plan to escape, but he didn't get far. He hoped to walk home and get away from the entire incident, but still carrying all the evidence, he would never make it.

For the first five minutes, he hid inside a trash can, but after assuring himself that they wouldn't find him, he got out and continued his walk home.

"The police stopped me and said I looked like the man who just robbed a gas station. They found the gun and the money, and I was busted," Fuentes explains simply. "I was so drunk they were laughing at me."

Arrested, booked and charged with assault with a deadly weapon and attempted murder, he faced at least 18 years in prison. That figure came from the trial judge at his arraignment, he said.

"Man, I was scared to death."

As much as he was scared, a letter he received in the jail from Juanita showed just the opposite.

"She said she'd been praying that God would take me to a safe place."

October 1994:

In California, political battle lines clearly marked the two sides of efforts to pass or defeat Proposition 187, a bill to cut aid and education to illegal aliens. Voters would pass the bill Nov. 4, but a U.S. District judge would put a hold on implementation of the law based on Constitutional issues. In international news, leaders of Israel and Jordan signed a historic peace truce. In Haiti, U.S. troops seized military weapons as they attempted to force Haiti's military leaders to turn over control of the nation to the deposed Jean-Bertrand Aristide, the winner of the nation's presidential election in 1990. The action came as a result of Haiti's military leaders ignoring demands from both the United States and the United Nations.

Chapter 6: A New Home – Prison

For a man who had taken great pains and expense upon himself and his family members to avoid life behind bars in Honduras, Fuentes now had a new home – one with bars and guards.

At the Orange County Jail, Ricardo Fuentes had a new name: H10762. When prison staff called out his last name, he always had to answer with the number 62, the last two numbers of his jail number.

His cellmates in Tank 28 included about 20 whites, 20 blacks and 20 Mexicans or folks from other Latin American and Asian nations. Although the Orange County Jail would remain his home for about eight months, the crowded cell would not. For some reason, the day after his arrival, the Hispanic cell population voted him president of the tank, or group cell – at least of the Hispanic population. That leadership was put to the test about a month after arriving in the cell. Unofficially, each of the three phones that inmates could use at times was set up on a segregated basis: white, black and others. When one of the black inmates used the "others" phone, disgruntled inmates demanded something be done. It was Fuentes' job to settle the situation with the black president.

"He was so big, but we had to fight each other," Fuentes says.

That fight pretty much turned into a small riot, and when all the commotion subsided, Fuentes was on his way to solitary confinement, or the hole, for forty-five days.

Literally and figuratively, from the hole he figured he had only one way to look, and that was up.

"From there I didn't have anything to lose if I try the Lord again, so I became a Christian in the hole," he decided. "I reconciled with God."

Someone had given him a Bible that he was able to take to his solitary confinement, and that helped as God waited for him to come to a true place of repentance, and not just try to bargain with him.

"I bend my knees, read my Bible, and say, 'God, if you really exist, take me out of this place and I will serve you.' I spent Christmas and New Years in solitude, and while everyone was celebrating, I was crying," he says. "Finally, I said, 'God, forgive me. You have spared my life many times already.'"

But as low as he found himself in the hole, he soon discovered worse places existed in the jail system. After Fuentes was released from solitary and returned to the general inmate population, a trip to the jail's hospital gave him a whole new view.

When they took x-rays and checked his lungs, they perceived that the scars left there from ingesting the insecticide when trying to kill himself as a young teen, as well as the ensuing TB, were in fact living tuberculosis. That meant he was contagious and a danger to the rest of the inmate population. His new home became a cell in the medical unit for about two months. After many more saliva tests and X-rays, staff decided the Honduran did not have TB and returned him to the regular inmate population.

"I was with crazy people and sick people," Fuentes says with a grin. "Man, I went from the hole to the hospital. I was not doing very well."

He spent eight months in the Orange County Jail, meeting monthly with prosecutors and his attorney. Prosecutors continued to tell him the best he could do was plea bargain for the 18-year sentence they said he'd get from the beginning.

Although he refused to accept and sign the plea bargain, inwardly he felt sure he'd probably face the 18 years in prison. He was convinced enough to write Juanita and tell her she should find another man and try to get her life back.

"I would not say anything other than to take care of the girls," says Fuentes. "She was already a Christian and sent a letter back saying, 'Don't worry, I am going to wait until you come back out of prison.' I was in tears because of that letter.

"Each time they offer me the same sentence. They said they had the video of me, gang members as witnesses and everything was against me," Fuentes recalls. "I was kind of lost and felt like I didn't have a choice, but they gave me a public defender."

Like many Christians feeling the heat of battle, he saw his future from two perspectives. The negative side said he'd face 18 years in prison, while the faith side welled up greater after each visit to the courtroom.

"I'd pray louder and louder, each time, until my heart was broke, I really meant it, I really wanted to do it," he says. "I started looking in the Bible, 'Speak to me, Lord. Talk to me, God, I want to hear your voice.'"

Another Christian told him to just start reading in the Bible and God would indeed speak to him directly. Being unfamiliar with the Bible, he just opened it up to start reading and found the voice of God speaking to him through the Old Testament prophet Isaiah in Chapter 54.

"Fear not, for you will not be put to shame; Neither feel humiliated, for you will not be disgraced; But you will forget the shame of your youth, And the reproach of your widowhood you will remember no more.

"For your husband is your Maker, Whose name is the Lord of hosts; and your Redeemer is the Holy One of Israel, Who is called the God of all the earth." (NASB)

He hung his mental, emotional and spiritual anchor to those verses, and they would prove to be an accurate assessment of his future. Fuentes gives credit to God for the short sentence the judge handed down, although he credits his public defender for representing him well.

"She did a pretty good job, but I believe the Lord did it," says Fuentes. "The next time I went to the judge, he said, 'I don't know what happened here, but the video doesn't seem very clear. They said the shotgun you were using is not enough to convict you for eighteen years. But you know what? You're going to spend five years.' The judge thought I was crazy because I fell down on my knees and started crying. I took the sentence as a sign the Lord loved me."

News in Honduras that Fuentes had landed in prison and would spend a number of years behind bars was received with mixed feelings. Although his father, Catalino, would end up missing his son during his life as an illegal alien and the ensuing incarceration in California, he believed things would probably be better for Fuentes in prison. He had already worked through the processes of worry when his son fled illegally to the United States, including the accompanying knowledge that he could be killed during the trip from Honduras.

"Being in reality, I got happy that he was in jail," Catalino said. "I got happy because I told my wife that nothing will happen to him while he is in that place. I told her they would take care of him, and he would learn a lot because he's smart."

For Amparo, Fuentes' mother, his time in prison brought both joy and bitterness of soul to her and Juanita.

"We were always praying to our Lord – praying and fasting," she recalled. "He would call us some times from prison, and we had a little joy ... sometimes we got sad. But together we cherished the joy and sadness too."

His letters too brought them joy, but the long interlude between some letters left them wondering and troubled.

Once Fuentes agreed to the plea bargain and the state accepted it, he found himself being shipped to another new home – Wasco State Prison, north of Bakersfield, California.

According to the Wasco State Prison website, the facility was the first of two identical prison and reception centers in Kern County, with the second located near the town of Delano. Both institutions have as a primary task the responsibility to provide the short-term housing necessary to process, classify, and evaluate new inmates physically and mentally in order to determine their security level, program require-ments and appropriate institutional placement.

That process typically takes no longer than six months, the amount of time Fuentes spent at Wasco.

Once he got to jail, Fuentes says he really did start seeking to serve God, even though years later he would see most of that time in prison as a period where he was really playing at being a Christian.

"I had a thought that when they were talking about sentencing me to eighteen years that God would help me," he recalls. "Now, other prisoners called me 'Punk' because I claimed to be a Christian. But I

prayed, 'God, I know I failed you, but I will really serve you this time."
God apparently took him at his word, for in the time spent at Wasco,
Fuentes encountered and used a number of opportunities to minister
to other inmates.

"Some prisoners would come to my cell and I talked to them about
Christ. Some wanted to hear about him and others didn't," says Fuentes.

People living under rough conditions such as prison or abusive families are known to put on hard exterior appearances, yet inwardly pos-
sess a much gentler makeup than the one others see. Such was the case
with one of Fuentes' cellmates in Wasco.

The two men would play chess as often as time allowed, which Fuentes commented, "We had a lot," and he would attempt to talk to him
about his need to know the Lord Jesus Christ. The man let Fuentes
know he wanted nothing to do with it, yet the day came when he
wanted his prayers.

"One day he requested that I pray for him. He said the night before
he had dreamed he was fighting against something and that it was killing him," Fuentes recalls. "He also said he watched me sleeping like a
baby, and he was fighting against this thing."

After the man asked his opinion what it all meant, Fuentes told him
that he thought the Holy Spirit was fighting against some bad spirits
the man had within him.

But his cellmate had emotional needs as well as spiritual, and they
were needs Fuentes well understood. Coming from another country,
they both had to deal with the fact that unlike many others in the
prison, no one came to visit them. Fuentes had his sister and nephews
in the States, and he did get a few letters from Juanita and his daughters, but not many visits.

"We have a saying in Honduras that if you are in the hospital or prison, you will know if you have friends," he recited. "I found out I didn't have any. ... That bothered me a lot at the time. It's true what they say that you don't know what you've got until you lose it."

But Fuentes did get some letters from the outside other than those Juanita and their daughters sent him. Once he discovered the prison literature ministry of the Kenyon's Gospel Publishing organization, based in Lynnwood, Washington, he not only received letters from the ministry's leaders such as Jim Dofelmier, but he also received books written by the late E.W. Kenyon that encouraged him in his faith and growth as a Christian.

Although his growth in God's ways and forgiveness got him past the regular nightmares drawing him back to the night he killed a man in Honduras, Fuentes still had plenty of dreams. But as he continued to try to serve his Savior from inside the bars of prison, the dreams changed to something far more pleasant.

"I had a couple different dreams," he remembers. "One was that I saw the Lord coming in the clouds just as the Bible says, and I dreamed that I was going with him. Twice I dreamed that on different days."

Serving God in prison can be easy and difficult at the same time, according to Fuentes. The easy part comes because at times there's little else for a Christian to do other than read the Bible and pray. Even when assigned to a work crew or a job inside the prison such as Fuentes landed, the term "serving time" means just that.

The difficulty in serving God in prison comes from the confined in tight quarters with those who want to use you to accomplish their goals, as well as with those who have no use for your beliefs ... particularly if they think you're less than 100 percent sincere. Looking back on his time in prison, Fuentes would later admit that he was not as sincere as he should have been during much of his time behind bars.

When he first arrived at the prison that would be his home for most of his sentence, fellow Hondurans offered him protection from the violence that has become a part of prison life. But that protection came with a cost – selling drugs inside the prison for them.

"In the beginning I helped them," he now says quietly. "I remember being in the middle of them and feeling alone, wanting someone to protect me."

As he gained the strength to stand more for what is right, some of his fellow inmates challenged his faith. They reminded him that he not only helped them sell drugs in prison, but was also arrested for assault with a deadly weapon and attempted murder.

"They'd say 'With what you did, why are you hiding yourself behind that Bible?' Sometimes I'd get mad, but I got used to hearing that from them," he says.

With 14 months behind bars, eight in the Orange County jail and six at Wasco, Fuentes would once again find himself living at a new address: Ricardo Fuentes, K10762, Soledad State Prison, California.

At Wasco, officials look at such things as the severity and number of crimes a convicted inmate has been sentenced for, as well as the convict's criminal history, in order to gauge which of the four security levels of prisons would be an appropriate assignment for new inmates. The 27 points assigned to Fuentes' record, or jacket, sent him to maximum security in Soledad. But as it turned out, he ended up fairly well off – for an inmate in a state prison.

Being able to speak fluent enough English to pass a GED test, Fuentes moved to the East Dorm where he would work for the Prison Industry Authority. Inmates called the area Disneyland because they had such privileges as earning money and being allowed to have such things as televisions, radios, jewelry and fans.

"At Soledad, it was the hand of the Lord, not luck," he declares emphatically. "I believe God had me in that place."

Prison work for Fuentes started out as a job on an assembly line sanding pieces of wood for office furniture such as desks and bookcases – earning twenty-five cents an hour. After two months he moved up to operating a sand blaster on metal parts for the welding shop. Three months later on that job, trouble with a civilian supervisor, or outmate as they're called, nearly led him back to his old ways.

The supervisor decreased his already meager pay, and that bothered him "for some strange reason." What bothered Fuentes most, he says, is that the man claimed to be a Christian.

The tension grew so much within Fuentes that he considered taking the man's life.

"I asked this Mexican dude from Texas named Bird how many more years in jail I'd get if I killed this man," he recalls. "He said, 'If they don't burn you in the chair, you will serve life. But first they will take you to the shoe cell ... That is where they will show you how to behave.'"

Word from the prison grapevine says that those who go to the shoe cell are stripped naked and chained hand and foot to a chair, and food is not served but once every two days. True or not, that was enough to dissuade Fuentes from continuing to dwell on any such plan.

"I decided not to kill him and to change my job," Fuentes says. "I went in back of the sandblasting machine and started praying for the Lord to change my mind. I was crying, and no one was watching. But I told the Lord that I didn't want to spend the rest of my life in prison."

God did send him help, but it came from the oddest direction. A man named Hector, who befriended Fuentes, helped him get a job in the upholstery shop, away from the supervisor with whom he'd been struggling. Hector, Fuentes would later find out, was serving time for raping a little girl with his brother.

Despite the channel through which the answer to prayer came, Fuentes was grateful not only for the change, but for his new supervisor. Manuel, or Manny as he was affectionately called, treated the men fairly and gained a lot of respect.

"Not that I'd ever want to, but if I had to go back, I'd want to work for him," says Fuentes. "He was a very nice man."

For some inmates, particularly for the alien population, life in Disneyland was better than what they'd left behind at home. In addition to the wages they received as working inmates, they got their three meals each day, cigarettes and regular family visits. Those perks, if that's what they could be called, kept fighting within the dorm to a minimum. No one wanted to be sent back to serve time with the general inmate population.

To Fuentes, the only real drawback to life at "Disneyland" was the lack of creativity on the menu. All inmates knew from day to day and meal to meal what they'd be eating. The weekly menu never changed.

Although Fuentes says he felt as though he played at being a Christian for most of his time behind bars, during his last year at Soledad that completely changed. Prayer, Bible study, witnessing and close personal times with his savior came to mean more to him all the time.

"I got tired of playing Christian and started being a real Christian," he says.

Inmate Christian services soon provided the opportunity for him to start preaching to more than just a couple people at a time. During one of the services, he says God spoke to his heart and gave him the Scripture verse from one of the Old Testament prophets, Isaiah. Found in the fifty-first chapter and fourteenth verse, he read, *"The captive exile hastens, that he may be loosed, that he may not die in the pit, and that his bread should not fail."* (NKJV)

When that time finally came for at least one captive to be set free, after more than five long years, Fuentes was ready to go in some ways but hesitant in others. While in prison, thoughts or concerns about the future are very limited. Now, knowing that he'd be deported to Honduras, he had no idea what awaited him. He could be stepping out of a prison with all the controls he'd grown accustomed to in the States during this stay, to a Honduran prison where newspapers and televisions were currently reporting that riots were taking the lives of inmates. He also didn't know how the blood feud with his knifing victim's family would play out.

He truly had no idea, but in the journey between Soledad and Honduras, he'd get an inkling of what would be in store for him. During the final stages of his incarceration, he was transferred from Soledad to Centinella State Prison for deportation classification, and then handed over by California State Prison officials to an immigration prison. One of the Christian inmates he spent time with during the transition prophesied over Fuentes and said that he would one day serve the Lord in front of the multitudes and that many people would come to know the Lord because of his testimony.

Before he could ever even consider getting to see the multitudes, let alone preach to them, Fuentes would first have to pass through the hands of U.S. immigration officials. Although the prisoners were assigned to crowded tank-like cells, just like the one where Fuentes started his prison sojourn in Orange County, everyone did their best to get along.

"No one wants problems there because they're so close to going home," Fuentes explained. "People don't want problems because they don't want to go back to the state prison again."

It was during his stay of about two weeks at the deportation prison that Fuentes got a taste of what God had in store for his future as he preached to groups of fellow inmates at church services where many of them would bring their own Bibles.

But after more than five years behind bars and getting ready to return to his native country, he'd definitely be leaving the known for an unknown world full of uncertainties.

March 2000:

In the nation of England, Chilean dictator Augusto Pinochet left a free man after 16 months of incarceration for human rights violations. The British government declined extradition requests from Belgium, France and Switzerland in its decision to set him free. In Mozambique, floodwaters trapped thousands of residents, and in the United States, George W. Bush and Al Gore won the presidential nominations from the Republican and Democratic parties.

Chapter 7: Free But Fearful

Shackled in chains while flying on board a commercial airliner from San Diego to Houston and then to Tegucigalpa, Honduras, Fuentes discovered that it was a little difficult to keep focused on a prophecy he'd received from a fellow prisoner in the deportation prison just days before. He'd been told that one day he would be preaching to the multitudes. The shackles also made it difficult to talk about Jesus Christ, his Savior, to others on the plane also being deported.

"They put me in chains, legs, waist and hands, because I was considered dangerous," Fuentes says. "I was talking with these guys on the plane about the changes in my life, yet they saw the chains. I knew God had made these changes, but they saw that I did something really wrong. I said, 'Well, we're all coming back to Honduras, all of us. What I did is in the past.'"

Getting released from Soledad brought joy indeed, but the thought of going to a Honduran prison upon his return to his native country brought dread. Although God had forgiven his past, the government of

Honduras and the family of the man he killed likely had not as far as he knew, and he'd likely have to face one or the other of them when he returned, or maybe even both.

According to Fuentes, reporters and television crews often gather at the airport when planes carrying deportees return to Tegucigalpa, and that was just what he didn't want to find. Having his face show up in the news for relatives of the dead man's family to see didn't seem like it would be a good idea.

"There's usually lots of reporters at the airport, and I didn't want to appear. I was scared," he recalls. "But I had prayed and told the Lord that I would serve him no matter what. There was not one reporter at the airport."

If the police arrested him at his return, Fuentes figured he'd spend another ten to twenty-five years in prison – if he lived that long. Prior to his flight back to Honduras, he had seen on television news about Honduran prison riots where the inmates were killing each other. Gangs within the prisons seemed to be creating the violence, and the display of tattoos he'd picked up along his path of destruction would likely cause one or another of the gangs to be against him.

"I was praying on the plane to the Lord to not allow the police to catch me. It was a very unusual prayer, but I had no choice," he states. "It's amazing that the Lord listened to me."

Before leaving the airplane, authorities removed his shackles, allowing him to walk out the door a free man of sorts. He still had to pass through the police officials at the airport's immigration station, and all their paperwork.

"They said, 'What's your name?' I didn't want to tell them, but it was in the papers anyway," he recalls with a grin. "I said in a prayer, 'Lord, be your will done,' and I gave them my name. They said, 'OK, you can leave.' I couldn't believe it; the police in my country didn't want me.

They gave me my freedom."

To Fuentes, it was as though he'd never killed the man. Exactly how things worked out he doesn't know, and it has left him with at least one unanswered question.

"It was not on the records, but I knew it was," he says excitedly. "The file was not there. I have to ask the Lord some day what he did with the file. He just kind of deleted what happened in the past."

Walking out the door of the airport, he now breathed the air as a free man – free from prison, free from old habits and free to serve the Lord.

But many issues still awaited his arrival.

When he left seven years before, his daughters were little girls, and now they were teenagers who had not seen their dad throughout their transition into young womanhood. Seven years had also been added to Juanita's life, some difficult years at best. And he still had no idea what to expect from the family that had once sought to kill him in retaliation.

And he and Juanita were still not married – something that would be remedied very quickly.

With $300 in his pocket from his last prison paycheck, Fuentes caught a bus for the long ride back to San Pedro Sula on a route still plagued by the damages Hurricane Mitch hammered on portions of Central America in November of 1998. Nicaragua and Honduras took the brunt of the hurricane, losing thousands of lives in each nation, as well as seeing the homes of millions of their people destroyed. During the hurricane, parts of Tegucigalpa were buried under 100 feet of water, and in San Pedro Sula, the waters sweeping out of the mountains toward the Port of Cortez left miles and miles of level farm and plantation land looking like one huge river.

Fuentes would find rough spots in the road of his future as well, but he'd committed his life to the Lord and figured the Lord would help him through whatever he faced.

A family member had rented a home to Juanita and her girls before Fuentes returned, one that was well away from the scene of the killing years before. Just arriving home after so many years, and to a home he'd never lived in, brought joy and difficulties.

But for Lucy, his eldest daughter, the night of his return was nothing less than joyous.

"We were all very anxious and waiting for the day he was coming. The family gathered together in our house waiting for his coming," she recalls. "Because it was late at night, I went to bed with my sister, and the rest of the family stayed awake, waiting. When he arrived, I heard singing, and we woke up and saw who was singing, and we saw that he was back and started crying and giving him lots of hugs and kisses.

"I was thankful to God because he allowed me to have my dad back home."

She admitted that they later ran into some difficulties just because he came back to find his girls had grown up while he was gone.

Daughter Kimberly likewise remembers the night her dad returned, but most specifically recalls thinking that she would not have to have another Father's day without her father.

Such a welcome overwhelmed Fuentes some.

"My woman and my two daughters were waiting for me. I didn't deserve them," he says. "When my daughters told me they missed me, I asked them if they missed the drunk man that used to hit their mom. They said, 'No, we know you are a new creation.'"

Juanita too rejoiced at her man's return, and had already set in motion the plans for their marriage – something they'd worked out through the letters they sent each other during his imprisonment.

Five years in prison builds many habits into inmates, and those aren't easily shucked when a man or woman walks back into a world of freedom. Without knowing it, the first meal Juanita served was the exact same meal inmates ate with great regularity, referred to by them as SOS. She also served him peanut butter, something on the menu every day during his stay at Wasco.

"I can't stand in front of a peanut butter jar," Fuentes says with a laugh.

Clothing presented another challenge.

"I was in blue for five years. When I came home to Honduras, Juanita bought me a couple pairs of jeans and a couple blue shirts," he said. "I threw them away and said I want to wear something else now."

Three years later, he'd finally grow accustomed to wearing jeans sometimes, but he's never forgotten how often he wore them in the past. He still wakes up daily at 5 a.m., just as he did behind bars for more than five long years.

Fuentes and Juanita ran into some conflict learning to be with each other. Just waking up during his first few days at home, he didn't know if he was home or still in prison.

"Believe it or not, you miss prison," he says reflectively. "You are so used to that place that you miss it."

He'd gotten used to polishing his shoes and making his bed every day, as well as ironing his clothes. In the years between Honduras and prison, he'd also gotten used to fixing his own meals. Juanita wanted to take care of those things now, and Fuentes had a tough time turning loose of those responsibilities.

Living in prison conditions, he'd learned to talk with other inmates about deep concerns as well as general topics, but always as men talk with men. Now he found it hard to talk to Juanita, and despite how much he had wanted to get home and be with her, he found himself giving her orders.

"I didn't have soft words for her," he explains. "I kind of lost my sensibility for talking with women."

Although it would take two weeks for him to venture from the safe environment inside his home, it took much longer before he could even sit without having his back against a wall.

"I didn't trust anyone, even out of jail," he recalls. With a laugh he remembers, "The first few months when I went to the barber, I asked where all the other guys were."

Despite his apprehension about leaving the house, one week after arriving home he had an appointment he had to keep.

"While I was in jail, we were talking all the time through letters, planning for the marriage when I got back." With a grin he added, "She got everything set up, I didn't have any choice."

The wedding truly was a family affair, owing to the fact that his finances were limited to what he returned with from prison, minus the bus fair home.

"The truth is, we didn't have enough money for the wedding party," he says. "Everything was given for free. It was a blessing."

One of the Christian brothers from church gave them the wedding bands, and his sister Josefa gave Juanita her wedding dress. One of his brothers gave them the wedding cake, and Fuentes' wedding pants came from Catalino, his father.

The wedding ceremony took place in the church where the pastor was Marcos Jordan, the man he would later be robbed and beaten with on their preparation journey to Huehuetenango, Guatemala.

"It was a big family wedding. There were many from my family and all her family was in the ceremony."

Other than the wedding, Fuentes stayed confined to his home for almost two weeks, but listening to a radio sermon one morning changed that.

"He was preaching about never giving up, no matter what you did in the past. You have to face reality ... and God will protect you no matter what you've done," Fuentes remembers. "I believe it was the word of God. He said, 'Even if you have killed someone, don't give up, the Lord has changed your life.'"

The message brought tears to his eyes, and he took courage. Although it would be two months before he'd return to his old neighborhood, the morning after hearing the radio sermon he told Juanita he was leaving the house to go look for a job. She cautioned him to be careful, and shortly after, Fuentes got a good look at the protection he'd heard about in that sermon.

Riding in a taxicab near one of San Pedro Sula's large Price Mart stores, he wore the dark sunglasses he'd bought in prison in order to not be recognized by the family that had been looking to kill him. Instead of running into those family members, he encountered gang members from some of the violent gangs that had surfaced in the city.

"They were riding in a small, white car and they were in front of my window, window to window. They pointed a rifle, I think an AK-47, and one of them told me this is the day I was going to die," Fuentes said. "I took off my glasses and said I wanted to know who was going to kill me. I was just waiting to die; I knew what I had done. I was ready to die."

God had plans for Fuentes, and either these gang members were simply trying to frighten the men in the taxi, or they found out they were powerless against those plans.

In the New Testament book of Revelation, Jesus Christ sent messages to the churches in Asia. In the third chapter, he said to the church in the city of Philadelphia, *"These things says He who is holy, He who is true, He who has the key of David, He who opens and no one shuts, and shuts and no one opens: I know your works. See, I have set before you an open door, and no one can shut it; for you have a little strength, have kept My word, and have not denied My name."* (NKJV)

God even shuts firing mechanisms.

Fuentes recalls, "I watched him right to the eye. He tried to shoot me, and the gun just didn't shoot. You could say it was luck, I say it was the Lord. The cab driver and I both thought we were gone, but I'm still alive. The gang members were just running and laughing ... we were in shock."

That day became a turning point for the ex-con.

"Since then I have no reason to be afraid," he declares.

Having gotten past the fears of returning to life as a free man, Fuentes and his new bride and daughters knew he needed to go to church for fellowship. Finding a church near their home opened up the first of many doors outside of prison for fulfillment of the prophecy he'd received about preaching to the multitudes.

"We attended the church for the first time as a family. I liked the environment there," he recalls. "A few days after that they allowed me to preach and testify about what the Lord did for my life. So I did it, and they just loved my testimony. We had very good fellowship with the brothers in that church."

That truly was just the beginning.

One morning shortly after his return to church fellowship, his brother-in-law invited Fuentes to attend a pastors' conference, even though he wasn't a pastor. After taking a seat in the back, he felt the Lord tell him to go to the president of the pastors association and tell him he was there to serve, and if they needed any help translating, he would be available to help.

"This man asked me, 'Who are you? Where do you come from? We don't need you, go back to your seat.' He was right. I was not trying to be important, I was just a son of God," says Fuentes.

The conference had scheduled some preachers from the state of Arkansas to address the gathering, and the president himself was a capable interpreter. But when the preaching started, the president found himself unable to speak and quickly motioned for Fuentes to come forward and help.

"I stood up, introduced myself to the brother preaching, and he prayed for me. I felt like a fire came upon me," he remembers. "Every word he preached I translated. Every move, every feeling, I also was there. It was a very successful message. All the pastors were yelling with joy. It had to be the work of the Lord."

After the meeting, many pastors asked for his phone number and wanted to know who he was and what church he was attending – including the son of his soon-to-be traveling companion, Marcos Jordan.

Not many days later, Fuentes went to the mountains with a group of Christian men for a week of fasting and praying. He remembers having one focus in his prayers – asking the Lord to allow him to serve Him as He promised while he was in prison. When he returned home he found a letter from Marcos Jordan telling him, "Brother Ernie, you have been chosen to interpret for William Smith in three crusades."

Smith was regarded by many pastors in Honduras and other parts of Central America as a famous evangelist. It turned out that Mike Evans, the interpreter from Belize that Smith normally used, at the last minute could not make the trip to interpret for the scheduled crusades. Although the pastors had a long list of other interpreters, none of them could make it to the crusades either.

"I just bent my knees there and praised the Lord," says Fuentes. "They were looking desperately for an interpreter, and the Lord brought one from jail just to serve them."

April 2000:

U.S. Attorney General Janet Reno directed armed federal agents to seize Elian Gonzalez from his relatives in Miami, Florida, enforcing a government order to return the boy to his father in Cuba. The boy had survived a late 1999 shipwreck of Cubans fleeing their country, and his relatives sought political asylum for him. Reno's decision added to the controversy being discussed worldwide. In Russia, the nation's leaders approved a revised version of the START II long-range nuclear armament reduction agreement, leaving it to the U.S. Senate to approve the revisions. In Peru, Alberto Fujimore failed to receive a majority of the presidential votes, forcing the nation into a runoff election between Fujimore and Alejandro Toledo. Toledo withdrew before the runoff election, saying he feared that Fujimore would use fraudulent methods to win.

Chapter 8: A New Life Indeed

From taking life to giving life, taking from others to sharing with others, and from thief to trusted companion: God's kingdom is filled with the regenerated dregs of the earth. And Ricardo Fuentes was no different. Little did he know how valuable his early school classes in English would prove to be in the hands of his Maker.

For Marcos Jordan, the pastor who would later share in the pain and abuse Fuentes received when the pair was robbed in Guatemala, the decision to line up Fuentes for the Oregon evangelist, Bill Smith, came from three simple reasons: He first heard about the man returning from California prisons from Juanita, Fuentes soon-to-be wife, and they planned to have him perform the wedding ceremony; he'd heard

Fuentes interpret at the pastors' conference; and quite simply, there appeared to be no other interpreters available for the work.

Regardless of his reasons, he remains confident he made the right choice in April of 2000.

"I am very amazed at how a sinful man can be changed by the power of God to serve Him." he says.

Although Smith, the evangelist slated to soon arrive in Honduras, would only find out about Fuentes' past during their 150-mile drive eastward along the Caribbean Sea from San Pedro Sula to Tocoa, he looked upon the converted man's availability as a God send.

When Jordan had contacted the churches in Santa Barbara about bringing a crusade to their city, they were skeptical at best, and with good reason. The last American that came for an evangelistic outreach had not arrived prepared with a good interpreter and the crusade flopped.

"They felt like it had been a waste of time and money," says Smith. "Marcos told them that was the least of the worries because I used a Belize pastor and we always work well together and travel together like brothers. There's no problem."

Jordan was only part right. Smith and Evans had worked together through the years, crossing through jungles, over rivers and even hugging the floor of their room in San Salvador, El Salvador while bullets pierced the walls during the revolution in that country. Those experiences had drawn the men close together. Evans never questioned Smith about his methods or plans and was always ready to go when Smith called him.

Until this time, that is.

"On the Wednesday before I was set to leave on Saturday, I got a call from Mike, saying 'Hey, I hate to tell you this, but I can't go,'" Smith recalls. "I told him I wanted him to call Marcus and tell him."

Smith says lightheartedly that Jordan went wild.

"Marcos isn't sleeping, having big-time troubles," he says with amusement.

He received an email from Jordan saying he wasn't sure what they would do, but suggested that in his own church after Smith arrived, they could try out this one man he'd recently heard at the pastors' conference. If that didn't work out, they could hope to find someone along the way.

That was good enough for Smith. He'd gotten used to being very flexible in his missionary endeavors throughout Togo, Africa, Central America and the northern reaches of North America.

Why not give this Fuentes guy a shot at it?

"When I got there, I was too dumb to know what was going on," Smith says. "But when he gets up to interpret, he always stands a little behind me and to the side. I noticed him making a lot of the same movements I did, and I thought that had to be a gift.

"After the service, Marcus came up to me and asked me what I thought. I thought he did a pretty good job. How was I supposed to know he was the 146th person on the list? I said, 'I think we can do this.'"

For Fuentes, the tryout at Jordan's church turned out to be as much a test of his nerves as his ability and calling to interpret.

"I couldn't stand in one place, I was trembling, nervous and all the time playing with the mic cord," he remembers. "But we finally did a good job and Bill said we could do this in Tocoa, San Pedro Sula and Santa Barbara."

Along the road to Tocoa, when Jordan was out of earshot of their car, Fuentes took Smith aside and gave him a basic overview of his life.

"I need to tell you something," Smith recalls Fuentes saying. "You may not want me to interpret for you, and that's OK, but you need to know this."

Sitting out in the hot Central American sun, Smith listened to the Honduran disclose his life of failures before meeting and following the God whom Smith came to preach about.

When finished, Fuentes said simply, "I'll understand if you don't want me to interpret."

"I said I'm comfortable and confident that somehow God is in all this," Smith remembers. "I want you to interpret for me."

Others may have made a different decision, but for anyone who had watched Smith through the years, his decision would come as no surprise. Even Mike Evans, his interpreter who had to back out at the last minute, became a Christian out of a devious past not much different than Fuentes'. For that matter, World Wide Crusades, Smith's organization, just sort of grew as though the wind was blowing it along over smooth, bumpy and sometimes turbulent ground.

While starting and pastoring a handful of churches in Alaska, Smith worked at times as a commercial fisherman on his own boat and at times as a logger. At one point while in Alaska, he hired on with a logging company to stand guard with a high-powered rifle over other timber cutters working in an area heavily populated by grizzly bears.

As an Assembly of God pastor, Smith was asked in 1974 to return from Alaska to his home area of Oregon to start a church in a timber town of about 2,500; about ten time larger than the community of Harlan where he grew up and started out raising his own family. When he returned to Oregon, he learned that the state district had postponed its plans for the new church, and officials asked Smith instead to return to his hometown to pastor for a while.

Needing to provide for his family, as well as pastor the small church in the coastal mountains, Smith returned to logging – that is until a log rolled off a log truck and crushed him as it hit the ground. After recovering enough to get out of the hospital and start ministering, he learned that district leaders had altogether closed the door of opportunity to start the church he'd been called from Alaska to start. When officials asked him what he wanted to do, Smith told them he felt drawn toward evangelism.

Although evangelism provides little money for those who minister, Smith started traveling with a singing group on a half-time basis throughout Oregon's coastal towns and even into Portland.

"They sang and I preached," he says.

But prior to being released from the hospital, Smith caught the first breeze of God's plans for his future. While walking in the hallway one night, he heard a man moaning in pain and asking for help. Smith made sure he got the help he needed and later learned the man had been living in the English speaking country of Belize in Central America since the time his wife died. Before her death, the couple had been farming near Redmond, Oregon, and he felt the need for some sort of major change after she died. Smith didn't think much about their conversation until later the same year when a man came to visit him and told him he was facing some problems and thinking about going to Central America. Smith gave him the address and phone number of the man he'd met in the hospital and that man too ended up moving to Belize.

Feeling a pull toward Belize, the following year Smith too made the trip, but not to live, rather to find out what God had in store for him there. Before he left, he sent a letter to the man who'd come to talk to him and then moved to Belize.

"When I got into Belize City and heard the name of the nearest town to where these guys moved, I bought a bus ticket to Dangriga. Just as the bus got there, here's this guy walking down the sidewalk reading my letter. He'd just picked it up at the post office," recalls Smith.

The following day, while sitting on the steps of the parsonage for the Assembly of God church and wondering where this would lead, he saw a woman and two young children coming down the street. He knew within himself, for God showed him he says, that they were the pastor's wife and children.

"I told her who I was and that I was from the U.S., and she asked, 'What are you doing here?' I said I didn't know," he recalls. "She started crying and said her husband was in Belize City and he wanted her to preach at the Wednesday night service. She'd said yes but was scared and had been praying for God to send someone to do that for her. 'You may not know why you're here, but I do.'"

That pastor turned out to be Mike Evans, and the two men grew to be very close friends. At one time they preached 30 straight nights together.

Returning to Oregon and his career of logging, Smith kept a steady pace at his work until in 1989 when he felt a strong pull toward Honduras – despite the fact that he knew nothing of the country and couldn't speak the least bit of Spanish.

Smith tells the story of what happened next in this way.

I called Mike and said I didn't understand it, but trust me, I feel called to Honduras, and I don't know why. I'll send money to you, catch a flight to Honduras and see what you can find out.

He hopped a flight and got there in the middle of the general council meeting of the Assemblies. He walked into the office and was told they were in the middle of the meeting, but he said he needed to talk to them now. When he was invited into the meeting, he said, "A guy in the States who preaches feels God wants him to come to Honduras, and I felt I needed to talk to someone."

The superintendent looked at him and said, "Isn't this strange? This meeting was called to organize a crusade in San Pedro Sula, and we don't know who to ask to come from the States, and you walked in on this very meeting."

And so it was that in 1990, Smith flew again to Belize and was joined by Evans for a flight to the crusade in San Pedro Sula where thousands of people came and heard the gospel of Jesus Christ. Many of those attending were changed by the power of God and observed a number of miracles in their presence.

Putting on that crusade and others cost thousands of dollars, and Smith was the major financial backer. When he returned from Honduras, he put together a non-profit organization, World Wide Crusades, as a way to reduce the tax load on the money he was earning and using for the crusades.

"Spending $10,000 to $12,000 for a crusade and having to pay taxes on it to boot was not fun," he explained. "I formed the organization so that myself and others could contribute to the ministry."

After joining Smith on the road to Tocoa and Santa Barbara, Fuentes too found himself part of an organization that would continue preaching throughout Central America and even consider returning to the African continent – just three weeks after being released from a California State prison.

Once they arrived at Tocoa for the crusade, Fuentes went to work, albeit pretty nervously.

"I have bad knees and was having a tough time getting up on the platform," Smith says with a smile. "He was shaking so bad I thought he was going to collapse."

God's anointing came over the two men in Tocoa just as it had at the pastors' conference only days before.

"He did a fantastic job," Smith declares. "It was a very powerful service, and I knew we had made the right choice. I saw his heart. He didn't put on or try to impress anyone, I just felt he had a right heart."

The first night of the crusade, Smith went down to pray with others who had come forward to the platform to ask for prayer, and not knowing any Spanish, he'd ask his interpreter what the people were seeking in prayer. One young woman caught Smith's attention.

"I asked him what the problem was with this girl, and she said she had a devil," he recalls. "We prayed for her, and it hit her like a hammer and she was on the ground. Five minutes later she got up and said it was gone."

At the crusade in Santa Barbara, following the one at Tocoa, Smith turned one of the services over to Fuentes so that he could share the testimony of what God had done for him. He remembers as many as 400 people rushing forward for prayer after Fuentes had finished. Of those who rushed forward, about 120 turned their lives over to the authority of the Lord Jesus Christ.

Another night of the crusade, Fuentes remembers some of those in charge of the crusade getting ready to cancel the night's gathering because heavy rains had started to fall.

He told Smith, "Look, Bill, the prophet Isaiah prayed and the rain stopped. Why don't we do the same?"

"I raised my hand and asked God to stop the rain, and he did."

Looking back at those crusades, Smith knows he made the right choice. He had already seen plenty of miraculous provision in his life in Alaska and travels through Central America and Togo, Africa. To him, Fuentes' appearance had all the marks of the hand of God providing for a need.

"The timing was incredible," he declares. "Mike was involved with building a school, and his time was limited. It just seemed like when he couldn't do it anymore, God sent another along.

"I can say without reservation that this guy has been transformed by the gospel. He would lay down his life for me, and I've trusted him with thousands of dollars and he accounts for every penny. ... He's more reliable than I am, and he's everything someone would want in an interpreter."

That trust has not changed between the two men.

"Since then, I have been together with Bill in El Salvador, Nicaragua, Guatemala and Honduras," says Fuentes. "All kinds of things have happened to us."

But the men were not together that day in May of 2002. And all the praise and confidence Smith had in his interpreter could not help him or Marcus Jordan as they lay beaten, battered and bruised in a forested area just ten miles from Guatemala City.

May 31, 2002:

The European Union with its 15 members jointly ratified the Kyoto treaty aimed at reducing levels of greenhouse gases blamed for global warming. In Colombia, a defeated Andres Pastrana blamed rebel forces for failing to work for peace, something he had promised to negotiate in his 1998 landslide election. Alvaro Uribe won the May election with a rightist, security and anti rebel stance. Also in Colombia, Pedro Carmona, the coup leader who for less than 48 hours replaced Venezuelan President Hugo Chaves as protests against Chavez turned violent, said from his Colombian asylum that he left to avoid a biased trial.

Chapter 9: Delivered From Death

The email Bill Smith received May 31, 2002 very simply explained the situation his interpreter Ricardo Fuentes and Honduran pastor Marcos Jordan had faced.

It read:

Dear Brothers.

May God continue blessing you all. Thank Jesus we are still alive to continue working for his kingdom.

Last Monday we left Honduras to Guatemala to organize Huehuetenango crusade for next November. Forty pastors were waiting for us, but during our drive to that place we were assaulted and robbed by thieves. Brother Marcos was with me; actually we were riding in his car. At the moment we were robbed, I was driving. The bandits were chasing us for many miles since they thought we were businessmen from Honduras. They claimed to be cops when they yelled at me to stop, but we decided not to stop and run for our lives. I pushed them out of the road for a few seconds, but they got really mad and shot at us. The car received three bullets, one of them hit my head. But thanks to a miracle of God I am still alive. It was about 6:30 in the afternoon and it was a little dark. Once I fell on Marcos legs he thought I was dead, but suddenly I recovered my senses and tried to run. The car was stuck and we could not avoid being caught. They took us to the woods and hit us with guns, asking us for the money. I was bleeding and a little confused. There was nothing to do anyway. There was four of them and they were armed to the teeth. It was an hour in agony while they took the money and other personal belongings, but thanks be to God they decided not to kill us.

They took $250 that was supposed to be used to pay preliminary expenses for the crusade, Marcos' watch, Marcos' reading glasses; Marcos' cell phone is missing. They took my watch, my wedding band, still photo camera, belt, penny bag and many other things I don't remember right now.

As another miracle, they did not take Marcos' car, but it is seriously damaged by bullets.

We are willing to go ahead with the crusade, but we will not drive a car through Guatemala again. We think to fly by plane or taking a bus are our choices.

Dear brothers, this was terrible, but greater is the one who is with us than the evil one. There are some things that need to be paid like my medicines and Marcos cell phone that we think is most important right now. Other things, let the Lord decide when to provide for us to pay them.

Our families are thankful to God for protecting us from death, but next time we are going to be careful.

I am recovering fast, as well as Marcos. You will have more info about the crusades soon. But now, please pray for us and God bless you all. If you can, please send money to replace the stolen money that we need for planning the church crusades.

Left tied, naked and bleeding on the forest floor, Fuentes seemed so lifeless that one of the bandits said he'd killed him, he recalls. Another disagreed and kicked him in the back just to make sure. He's convinced the men had done this type of robbery before because they would not refer to each other by name, only calling each other "Partner."

Jordan himself finally had to ask Fuentes if he were still alive, to which he could only reply with some sort of vague sound. With the pain and confusion, Fuentes is unsure just how long they were on the ground, other than to define it as a very long night. Although he's not positive, he believes he remembers hearing the bandits say that the police were in on the robbery and that they were told to kill their victims.

The bandits also accused the men of being drug dealers and demanded all the money they had or they would be killed. After they pulled his wallet from his back pocket, they started to call Fuentes by his name, calling him Mister. After rifling though Jordan's belongings and finding a little more money, they were still not satisfied.

"They asked if I was ready to die, and I did not answer that question immediately," Fuentes said. "They asked me that if that is all the money we had, why did we fight so hard. At that moment I thought they were right."

The bandits continued to kick their two captives, demanding more money and taking particular vengeance on Fuentes, accusing him of trying to kill them by pushing them off the road with his pickup.

"They asked me a second time if I was ready to die, and after crying for my life a little I started reciting Psalm 91," says Fuentes.

He who dwells in the secret place of the Most High Shall abide under the shadow of the Almighty. I will say of the Lord, "He is my refuge and my fortress; My God, in Him I will trust." Surely He shall deliver you from the snare of the fowler and from the perilous pestilence. He shall cover you with His feathers, And under His wings you shall take refuge; His truth shall be your shield and buckler. You shall not be afraid of the terror by night, nor of the arrow that flies by day, nor of the pes-

85

tilence that walks in darkness, nor of the destruction that lays waste at noonday. A
thousand may fall at your side and ten thousand at your right hand; but it shall not
come near you. Only with your eyes shall you look and see the reward of the wicked.
Because you have made the Lord, who is my refuge, even the Most High, your dwell-
ing place, no evil shall befall you, nor shall any plague come near your dwelling;
for He shall give His angels charge over you, to keep you in all your ways. In their
hands they shall bear you up, lest you dash your foot against a stone. You shall tread
upon the lion and the cobra, The young lion and the serpent you shall trample un-
derfoot. "Because he has set his love upon Me, therefore I will deliver him; I will set
him on high, because he has known My name. He shall call upon Me, and I will
answer him; I will be with him in trouble; I will deliver him and honor him. With
long life I will satisfy him, and show him My salvation." (NKJV)

"They told me to shut up. Brother Marcos was praying too, and they
told him to shut up."

After finding the American currency Jordan had hidden in his socks,
the men calmed down but still demanded their watches, glasses, penny
bags, wedding rings, belts, passports and other documents and camera.

"After they counted the money and split it up among themselves, they
said they were going to spare our lives, but we shouldn't be fools because someone would be watching us for two hours. And if we moved,
he would kill us both," Fuentes remembers.

Jordan remembers feeling the presence of God during the ordeal, and
he remained confident that he would live. But he was concerned about
Fuentes because of the bleeding from the bullet wound to his head.

"After six or eight minutes, I asked him if he felt good enough to get
out of that place, and he told me to wait more time because if we left
too early, the bandits could still be in the area," Jordan recalls."

The bandits had used the men's shoelaces to tie their hands and then
scattered their clothes around the forest to make sure it would take

them a while to gather things up after they freed themselves. They also tossed the pickup keys into the woods.

Jordan figures he and Fuentes stayed still for about a half hour before they untied their bonds and started moving. It took them some time to find their clothing and keys, but it would take them even longer to get their vehicle back to the highway.

"I had a terrible headache, our bodies were ground, but we were still alive," says Fuentes. "The car was like cheddar cheese with holes all around, but after what happened to us, the night was so calm and nice. We were alive and thanked God we survived this nightmare. ... The worst was over."

It took the men all the strength they had left to push the car out of the bushes and forest because the bandits had left it downhill from the road and over rough terrain.

"It took a huge effort to get the car out of the bushes, and it was with the hand of God pushing because I had no more power in me. But something inside me kept me pushing the car while Brother Marcos was trying to drive the car out of that place," said Fuentes. "Finally we did it."

Once on the road, confusion had the men divided in their opinions as to whether to return to Honduras or finish the drive to Guatemala City. For that matter, Jordan wasn't even sure which way to drive no matter what they decided.

Heading off to what they believed would take them to Guatemala City, just a few minutes later they encountered police officers who called an ambulance to take Fuentes to the hospital.

Just how close to death the two men were can be seen from a similar incident in late March of 2003.

Todd Fields, a missionary with Global Outreach International working in Honduras, died after taking three bullets while trying to avoid a similar robbery and trying to force the bandits' car off the road. Fields had been driving a van with two other adult missionaries and five high school missionary students along the Pan American Highway. The group was headed to a retreat at Guatemala's Lake Atitlan. According to reports from survivors of the robbery, these bandits also tried to drive the vehicle from the highway into the forest, but this one got stuck between two trees. They found little to steal and were angry, not only because their victims had little money, but also because they'd killed the driver, apparently ruining whatever other plans they had.

For Fuentes and Jordan, after being released from the Guatemalan hospital, they returned to their homes in San Pedro Sula. Doctors at the hospital later told pastors who had been waiting in Huehuetenango that it was just a miracle that Fuentes had walked out of the hospital because the bullet had stopped in his skull just decimeters from his brain.

At home, Juanita knew something bad had happened to her husband when he came back with his clothes dirty and filled with blood. She remembers seeing him missing one shoe, his watch and wedding band and having a set of stitches in his head where doctors had removed the bullet.

That experience sometimes leaves her a little afraid when her husband leaves to organize crusades and even preach without Smith, but she always grows thankful to the Lord when he returns home, she says. Fuentes and Jordan twice again traveled the path they'd taken the day they came so close to death, making it to Huehuetenango to help pastors organize the crusade that Smith came to hold in February 2003.

"Because of what happened the first time, we were very nervous, but it was a good testimony when we got to the pastors meeting because they told us how much they'd been praying for us," Fuentes says. "It brought happiness to the Christians, knowing God had protected us from death."

Smith, Fuentes and Jordan would like to be able to point to something positive about the robbery, such as a massive turnout with many conversions and miracles at Huehuetenango, but as yet they have no such thing. Smith says that although the crusade was one of the most organized at which he's preached, the turnout was less than even local pastors had expected. But it did have an impact on the area, he says, leading some people to Christ and healing some of those in need, as well as encouraging the local pastors and congregations.

A number of factors may have added to the low turnout, such as a nationwide teachers strike, loss of power and water in Huehuetenango for almost the entire day before the crusade's first night and a tendency for people in the area to stretch a scheduled 7 p.m. start to as late as 9:30. But probably more significant, Smith sees the fact that Guatemala is one of the more prosperous countries of Central America as also affecting the results. Prosperity and self-sufficiency tend to keep people from seeing their need for a savior or admitting it, he says.

Additionally, such things as the robbery of Fuentes and Marcos, as well as the death at the hands of bandits of the missionary accompanying teens to a retreat, point to spiritual warfare trying to keep the gospel of Jesus Christ from penetrating the country, Smith says.

With radio coverage of the Huehuetenango crusade, however, the gospel reached farther than just the northern portion of Guatemala. A group from the nearby Mexican state of Chiapas heard the radio broadcast and hired a bus to make the journey to Huehuetenango the following night. Unfortunately, they arrived so late the event had already ended for the night. But before turning around to head home, they asked Smith to come to their area and hold a crusade. Smith's driver and guide in that area has been to Mexico seeking to find the group and so far has not been able to locate them. But he will continue looking for them, Smith says.

A second crusade in Guatemala set for the town of San Pedro Soloma saw better responses from the locals. On the first night, the people pouring into a freshly cut cornfield, watered and packed down by hands and feet, would see at least one miracle.

During the service, a baby stopped breathing and the mother began to panic. The pastors and people gathered around them and began to pray. After a while, the baby again began breathing, and the people rejoiced over what the Lord had done.

In his life of preaching about the Kingdom of God, Smith has seen many others receive a new breath of life, just as the small child did in San Pedro Soloma. Sometimes it's been physical life or healing, but the majority of the time it has been the kind of new spiritual, emotional and moral life he's seen in Ricardo Fuentes.

And he has no plans to stop preaching. Likewise, Fuentes has no plans to stop translating.

John 8:32, 36

And ye shall know the truth, and the truth shall make you free…if the Son therefore shall make you free, ye shall be free indeed. (KJV)

Chapter 10: What Happens Now?

An old logger, pastor and evangelist who says alcoholic drink has never passed his lips ... a younger middle-aged man who spent his entire teen years and early twenties working his way toward prison on a fast slide headed for an early entrance to Hell. An odd couple for sure, but one newspaper reporter once wrote that they worked together like a fine two-cylinder engine, firing out the Word of God one right after the other.

The path from heartache to joy, spirit of heaviness to garments of praise and ashes to beauty was spread with headache and heartache for the man known as Ricardo Fuentes, for his family and for his victims.

Now, as he goes before Smith to prepare for crusades throughout Central America, he travels as an ambassador for his savior, Jesus Christ, the one who transformed his life. Together, the two men and those accompanying them have seen miracles of changed lives – spiritually, emotionally and physically.

In the Nicaraguan town of Jalapa, several thousand men, women and children broke through the fear that had enveloped the town since post-election riots to find themselves singing, crying, laughing and dancing with one another before the Lord.

In El Jicaro, Nicaragua, as many as 15,000 people gathered nightly on a soccer field overlooking much of the town to join in and listen to four hours of singing, testimonies, preaching and prayer. Many of those walked for hours to arrive, stood the entire service, and then walked home in the dark. By the last night of the four-day crusade, people packed like sardines in a can drove on a bus for hours from the larger town of Matagalpa to attend.

In La Palma, El Salvador, in addition to the hundreds of people who'd given their lives to the lordship of Jesus Christ, at least two women were miraculously healed from whatever had them confined to the life of cripples. Smith, Fuentes and their traveling companions might not have known of the healings were it not for a vehicle break-down. The plan had been to head to the capital city of San Salvador after the crusade to pick up a journalist who had flown in to catch up with the group. While attempting to make roadside vehicle repairs, Smith felt God wanted him to return to La Palma. When they again arrived, they heard people talking about the miracle lady.

Asking around, they found that a woman whose body had been left in a deformed and constricted following a stroke now walked as a whole woman. She had been carried into the meetings in a resin chair to ask for God's healing, and while nothing happened at the meeting, the following morning she found she was not only able to rise up from her bed, but she had been fully restored to her pre stroke condition.

But more important to Smith, Fuentes and those who travel with them are the people who have been delivered from lives bound up by such things as drugs, alcohol and gang life, with their accompanying consequences of destroyed lives and destroyed families … and ulti-mately eternal death.

Rebuilding a family so ripped apart physically and emotionally as the one Fuentes had created doesn't come easy they conclude, but through obedience to God's Word and the Holy Spirit, it can be done.

"In these three years since I got out of prison, I have learned how to love Juanita in a different way," he says. "When we don't know Christ, we're always looking for young, elegant, pretty women. I came from five years in prison and there were all those beautiful girls in the street, and I struggled for the first year. Now I'm very sure my love for Juanita is very real. It's the love that God can just put in your heart."

Despite the tough times the family went through when Fuentes left and the struggles to rebuild relationships, the journey has been worth it.

"I believe he left for the better," daughter Kimberly said, "because when he was living here with us, he wouldn't change like he has now. I am very happy."

To Josefa, Fuentes' sister who now pastors a church near the home where she and her brother grew up, the transformation she's seen in her brother has been a complete change. What she sees him doing now with his life fulfills a dream she had of him when he first returned to Honduras. In the dream she saw him clothed like a pastor and running very fast.

The experience the family went through also has left her more attentive to the needs of others around her. She's regretted being too busy during the days he most needed help – those following the stabbing death.

"I saw that he looked confused and wanted to talk to me," she recalls. "I was a brand new Christian, busy attending some customers and didn't pay attention. I always remember that, and that hurts me a lot, all the time.

"The Lord tells me again and again that people need attention of other people. Now, when I see someone that needs to be listened to, I put apart all that I'm doing and pay attention to those people."

The complete change in Fuentes' life continues to impress Smith.

"I think what's stood out is his work ethic for the Lord," he says. "He gets things done."

Smith points to an August 2002 crusade organized by Fuentes for World Wide Crusade as an example. Instead of Smith traveling to Honduras, Frank Fraga, an Assembly of God preacher from Sisters, Oregon went in his stead.

Fuentes once again had worked with church leaders in Chapalapa to get ready for the crusade.

According to pastors from the town, 136 people became Christians during the crusades. When the Sisters pastor returned home, he championed fund-raising efforts for a new church in that town. With the efforts coordinated in Honduras by Fuentes, that church which seats 400 people opened in December during a dedication with both Smith and Fuentes present.

"Ultimately it was he who got the supplies ordered and the materials," Smith says. "To me, that's what's proven him, his willingness to sacrifice, and he doesn't complain."

Smith says he sees irony in the fact that many would have difficulty with trusting a man with Fuentes' past with the sums of money he sends him to oversee.

"That's the evidence of the gospel of Jesus Christ as I know it," he explained. "I see too many people making half-hearted attempts to live for God. They have good intentions but don't understand you don't bargain with God."

The kind of transformation that allows Smith to entrust time, energy, money and the well being of others to Fuentes should be more common, according to Smith.

"God says we will find him when we seek for him with our whole heart. That example of someone who is completely broken before God and that kind of evidence is the kind I wish the non-Christian world could see. Like his experience, it wouldn't leave any doubts in their minds about the transforming power of God.

"I think that ought to be the result of every believer's life, where their integrity and work ethic doesn't need to be questioned – they can be trusted. Sadly, that's not true in many cases."

The kind of commitment Smith sees in Fuentes hasn't escaped the eyes of leaders in the Honduran Assembly of God, according to Smith. The organization recently granted Fuentes pastoral credentials without his having attended its Bible College – something virtually impossible in that country.

"They wanted him to go, but he didn't have the time and he had a family," Smith recalls. "He wanted to know what I thought, and I told him to trust God and keep serving him faithfully. They granted him credentials without going to their school. He may be the only one to ever have had that happen."

Having gotten to know Juanita, Smith sees the same type of commitment.

"I admire his wife as well. The testimony that she's had, willing to stick with him while trying to survive with two little girls waiting for him," he says. "She could have found someone else, but she didn't. I suppose a lot of credit should go to her for praying him into the kingdom."

The times that Smith and Fuentes have spent together, much like those times Smith spent with his former interpreter, Mike Evans, have bonded the men in a special way – the way that only shared laughter, tears, dangers and struggles can. That sort of bonding tops Smith's list of experiences in life. Working with a man so drastically changed adds to that pleasure.

"He just knows God is bigger than we are. His faithfulness and work stand out, and the contrast in his life between what he used to be with what he is now is like darkness and daylight," he says. "Such a contrast: a bitter, angry, mean, alcoholic, drug addict who was worthless has been totally changed by the Gospel. This is not a game, not religion, nothing but the miraculous transformation by the gospel of Jesus Christ."

Although Smith says the name of World Wide Crusades has probably grown bigger than it ought to, the organization has started 26 churches in Honduras, as well as two in El Salvador. Some of those churches display the World Wide Crusades logo right next to the Assembly of God logo. Crusades have reached into Guatemala, Mexico and Nicaragua. Smith, so far, has turned down an invitation to bring a crusade to the hostile regions of Columbia, but Fuentes set off for Costa Rica in late August 2003 with plans to work with pastors there to schedule crusades just prior to Christmas the same year. In January 2004, Fuentes set off for Ecuador to arrange another crusade later in the year. Plans are being laid for another 2004 crusade to reach out to the growing Spanish speaking population in Belgium.

Smith would like to see some way developed to make sure those churches the ministry helped start gain stability through training and discipleship. For now, pastors of the new churches receive a small salary for six months, allowing them to provide for their families while they build new congregations.

Smith doesn't know what the future holds for Fuentes, but he's confident the man will see more of the world than he's already seen.

"His vision is not limited to Honduras or Central America. His vision goes to Argentina, Africa, it's unlimited," he says. "You would think a Spanish speaking guy would limit himself to Spanish speaking countries. But he'd go anywhere with me at the drop of a hat."

For Fuentes, a man who found little reason for joy in his former lifestyle, the opportunity to interpret for Smith provided a good beginning for the joy that can be seen in him today. It also provided the opportunity to see for himself the joy God was developing in his life.

"I remember when I was hired to go work with Bill and I was asked how much I'd charge," he says. "Not a cent was my answer. I felt at that time that I was very joyful because I was doing what this brother prophesied in prison. I really knew then that my life had been changing for good."

"It's hard to believe that the Lord can help a killer, but with me he did it. Moses too," Fuentes concludes. "He wants me to serve him. The Bible is about second chances."

Matthew 28:19
Go ye therefore, and teach all nations, baptizing them in the name of the Father, and of the Son, and of the Holy Ghost. (KJV)
Mark 16:15
And He said unto them, Go ye into all the world and preach the gospel to every creature. (KJV)

Chapter 11: World Wide Crusades

Using the services of Bill Smith and the man known as Ricardo

Working with an interpreter in Guatemala, Bill Smith, head of World Wide Crusades preached to about 1,500 in one meeting in 2004. Smith says he never knows what to expect when it comes to attendance. It can be in the hundreds, or as large as the 12,000 people who showed up in El Jicaro, Nicaragua in 2001.

Fuentes, as well as many others attached to the World Wide Crusades organization, God keeps expanding the ministry and its outreach. While recently looking through a group of photos from Central America, Smith picked up a picture of two fishermen in a lone boat in the midst of Lago de Nicaragua (Lake Nicaragua) and gazed at it for several moments. The photo showed one man rowing the boat and the other casting his net into an endless horizon of blue water. It had been taken during a short respite from travels prior to crusades in northern Nicaragua.

"That's kind of how it felt when I first started here," Smith commented thought-

When World Wide Crusades holds events in the rural towns of Central America, men, women and children travel to the meetings in and on most anything imaginable – from walking and on bikes to riding on horses or donkeys. Others arrive in ox cart, donkey cart, buses or crammed like sardines into cattle trucks such as this one preparing to leave El Jicaro, Nicaragua in 2001. Some people will travel for hours to get to the meetings, stand for as long as three or four hours during the meetings, and then travel for hours to get home.

fully, "all alone casting a net for souls."

Although numerous church organizations and denominations existed and actively preached the gospel in the region before Smith started traveling to Central America, he still felt alone in the early days of his calling to minister in that part of the world. But that's no longer the case. Even while Smith is home taking care of pastoral duties in the Oregon coastal mountain town of Alsea, others continue to heed the ministry's call to go and preach the gospel.

The Honduran gospel band known as Eben-Ezer, working under the banner of World Wide Crusades, spent many days on the road holding crusades during 2003. Although the band members are all family men, mostly self-employed businessmen, they held more than forty-five days of crusades in nineteen towns throughout Honduras and Nicaragua. In addition to at least 2,700 people surrendering their lives to the Lord Jesus Christ during the crusades, many people witnessed miracles and saw restoration and revival breaking out in their communities and churches.

To date, World Wide Crusades has been responsible for helping start and supporting twenty-six new churches in Honduras and two in El Salvador. From Smith's first trip to Belize, the crusade's ministry has reached out to minister in El Salvador, Honduras, Nicaragua, Guatemala, Costa Rica and Ecuador. Although Smith doesn't know for sure what God has yet in store for World Wide Crusades, opportunities continue to open to the ministry. He was asked to preach in 2004 to the growing Spanish-speaking population of Belgium, as well as be part of year-long Year of Evangelism sponsored by the Assembly of God church in Honduras. He's likewise considering a return to Togo, Africa, one of his earliest stops as an evangelist.

Fuentes himself has been asked to travel to South Korea to preach. One of Smith's sons, a professional videographer, traveled to Honduras in early 2004 to produce an educational film on the growing AIDS epidemic in Central America. Numerous ministries and pastors plan to use the film.

After Hurricane Mitch devastated Honduras and Nicaragua, World Wide Crusades joined many other evangelical groups to travel to the region to hold medical clinics and help rebuild homes, churches and businesses, as well as preach the gospel to the multitudes living through the aftermath of the catastrophic event.

Likewise, the Jesus Broadcasting Network in Honduras asked Smith to be involved with their ministry through creating weekly sermons for airing not only in Central America, but also South and North America, Europe and Northern Africa.

Along the road of evangelism, the ministry has been involved with numerous medical and dental clinics held in some of the region's poorest areas. Numerous ministry supporters have been involved with helping construct church buildings for new congregations – cinder block by cinder block.

Regardless of how large or small

101

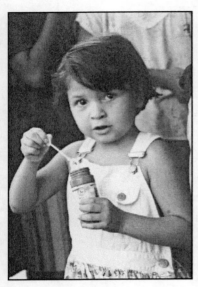

In an extremely poor barrio of San Pedro Sula, Honduras, it didn't take much to entertain children waiting for their turn to be examined by a doctor and receive needed medicine and prayer. Often in such areas where unemployment can run as high as 70 percent, simple treats such as soap bubbles just don't exist.

the ministry of World Wide Crusades grows, the message Smith and all those involved with the ministry deliver remains the same.

God came to earth in the form of his only born son, Jesus Christ, to provide the only acceptable payment for all our sins through his sacrificial death on the cross. Those who believe that message are guaranteed eternal life in his eternal kingdom.

They're also guaranteed that in accordance with his word, the Holy Bible, his Holy Spirit will take up residence in their lives to lead, direct and comfort them as he takes them into the most abundantly fulfilling life possible on this earth, one that's free from the sins that hold men and women in bondage

Crowds typically swarm to the temporary stage for prayer and worship following preaching by Bill Smith and his interpreter.

throughout the world – and one that's in agreement with his word.

If you are interested in such a life, the solution is simple. If, with all your heart, you recite the following prayer to God, he will transform your life into a life that is truly pleasing to him.

Dear God, I confess that I am a sinner in need of a savior. I have disobeyed the moral laws you not only wrote in the Bible, but even those you wrote within my own heart.

Thank you for paying the price for my sin through your death on the cross, and thank you for your promises of eternal life and the presence of your Holy Spirit in my life. I now ask for that forgiveness that you have offered, and I desire to turn control of my life over to you. Please take me and change me into the person you want me to be. Please empower me to live a life that is pleasing to you and not

Bill Smith prays for a man who came forward following a crusade meeting in Huehuetenango, Guatemala in 2004. Smith and other team members meet with as many of those seeking prayer as they can.

Outside the city of San Pedro Sula, Honduras, new believers in the Lord Jesus Christ meet for a baptism service held in a river already swollen from heavy rains. Bill Smith, second left in back wearing a white shirt, was joined for this service by San Pedro Sula pastor Marcos Jordan, standing next to Smith.

103

one that is set on pleasing myself. I want to serve you as my living lord and savior for the rest of my life. I thank you in Jesus name, Amen.

If you have prayed this in sincerity, or even if you haven't but you have questions you'd like answered about this life, please contact the pastor or leaders of a local Bible-believing church. If you don't know of any in your area, please feel free to contact

On a return trip to check out the work of an orphanage supported by World Wide Crusades in Jalapa, Nicaragua, team members take a short respite after hours of travel over rough roads from El Jicaro.

**World Wide Crusades
PO Box 9,
Alsea, OR, 97324;**

or by email at revbill@casco.net.

A resident of El Jicaro, Nicaragua solders together a string of light bulbs for night lighting on the dirt soccer field overlooking the town. When World Wide Crusades team members enter such rural towns, employment often increases drastically, although temporarily, as idle people are hired to help prepare the crusade site, transport people to the meetings, and prepare food and provide lodging for the team.

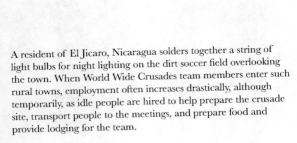

ISBN 141202573-7